Dedicated to the principals, teachers, and school personnel across America who teach and care for children...you are heroes.

 The Center For Teacher Effectiveness
4381 English Point Road
Hayden Lake, ID 83835
info@timetoteach.com (e-mail)
www.timetoteach.com (website)
www.goteachergo.com (website)
(tel.) 208-772-0273 (fax) 208-762-7026

cte Center For Teacher Effectiveness

Published by
The Center For Teacher Effectiveness (CTE)
4381 English Point Road
Hayden Lake, ID 83835

Visit us on the WEB!
www.timetoteach.com
www.goteachergo.com

Printed in the United States of America

September 1994,95,96,97,98,99,2000,01,02,03,04,05

FRONTISPIECE

Time, it has been said, is the coin of learning. Yet every teacher has known the frustration of losing valuable instructional time to matters of discipline, just as every student has known the frustration of losing valuable learning time to matters of discipline. For some teachers and for some students, the amount of time lost is very great. This book describes a program proven to restore that lost time to teachers and students in a way that is simple, fair, and mutually respectful. We believe that it can be effective for you in your unique situation. We have set out to explain it to you as clearly as we can, in the hope that it will help you expand your "time to teach."

Rick Dahlgren
Judy Hyatt

ABOUT THE AUTHORS

Rick Dahlgren is well-known nationally and internationally for the practical value of his published materials, and for his powerful presentations to teachers at workshops and conferences. He is a very dynamic educator who has published numerous books for teachers and parents over the past decade. **Rick Dahlgren has worked with tens of thousands of new and experienced teachers to help them develop strategies for dealing with challenging students in their own classrooms!** His experience in elementary, middle, and high schools, as well as at the university level, have helped him develop very innovative ideas which are helping teachers everywhere. He regularly presents at national, regional, and local conferences and for schools and districts and his seminars always receive universal praise.

Judy Hyatt has been a classroom teacher of English and Language Arts since 1960. She has taught in rural and urban high schools, an inner city junior high school, and – for the past 22 years – a small town middle school. In addition to teaching, she has been active in amateur theater, human rights, and her professional association. In 1993 she was chosen Coeur d'Alene, Idaho's, Teacher of the Year. In 1995 after attending an in-service presentation and meeting Rick Dahlgren, she began piloting Time To Teach! in her own classroom; concurrently, other teachers in the district did the same, and today the program is used with great success at all levels throughout her district.

Carolyn Dobbins is a "teacher's teacher." During her more than thirty years of teaching, her classroom has often been the place where new and prospective teachers visit to learn from her. She has left her mark. Those who know her best can attest to the fact that she is often stopped in shopping malls, parking lots, grocery stores, etc, by excited former students. "I will never forget," or "Do you remember the time. . ." crescendo off their lips like gathering winds, and the excitement grows as they talk. To say that students love her and appreciate what they were taught is to utter an understatement.

A dynamic speaker, she graciously shares with fellow educators useful and practical strategies to improve the classroom environment in a dynamic way.

FOREWORD

Research as well as daily headlines proclaim that aggressive and violent behaviors are increasing among children and youth in America's schools. We are all alarmed by the increasing numbers of youth who confront their parents, teachers, and school personnel with persistent, threatening, and destructive behaviors. In the aftermath of recent tragedies in American schools, it is all too clear that violence corrodes the educational process and threatens the safety of both students and teachers.

We do not pretend to have the secret to preventing such tragedies, whose causes are multiple and complex. But we do believe that good disciplinarians – at home and at school – promptly address minor problems in order to prevent major ones. Contemporary teachers realize that good discipline begins with the "little stuff." Yet, there is very little research or attention focused on the low-level behaviors impacting every classroom almost every minute of every day – and often preceding far more challenging and aggressive behavior! We feel that such neglect must be corrected. This program shows how prompt attention to the "little stuff" can prevent the "big stuff" – that is, how good timing is the key to effective discipline.

"Time To Teach" is an evidence based program. For nearly four decades we have exhaustively investigated the literature, as well as the teachings of other professionals. We also draw from our own observations, experiences, reasoning, and from what we have accepted from reading and studying all of the research on effective child management. We will provide theory to give you an understanding of low-level behaviors, and how they impact students and teachers. We will also provide techniques to demonstrate how those behaviors can be eliminated. Additionally, the techniques will help you manage a wide range of behavioral challenges with confidence and satisfaction.

TIME TO TEACH!

CHAPTER 1

TIME TO REFLECT ON OUR BELIEFS

Belief #1: Times have changed.

Anyone old enough to have a teaching certificate is aware of the many ways in which life has changed for American kids. The past fifty years have brought rapid changes in family structure, in our knowledge base, in technology, in the media, in demographics, in political decision-making, in economic and class structures, in parenting and in pedagogy. The consequences of these changes are varied and complex.

Many outcomes of the change are positive. For example, most students today are light-years ahead of those in the fifties in terms of how much they know and what they can do. (Judy and her teaching teammates agree that their seventh-graders are writing papers and designing projects far beyond anything that they themselves did even in high school.) Because formerly taboo subjects are being addressed, today's kids are also much better equipped to protect themselves from social ills like addiction, sexual abuse, racial discrimination, etc. And thanks to tremendous strides in pedagogy, their teachers can call on a wealth of research-based strategies to ensure that learning is really taking place.

Of course, there is a debit side. For whatever reasons, from exposure to mass media to distraction by family problems, today's kids do not always pay attention as well as their grandparents did. Certainly, they are not always as compliant as their grandparents were in the classrooms of yesteryear, when teachers listed major problem behaviors as "talking out of turn, inappropriate noises, chewing gum in class, not putting paper in the waste basket, and running in the halls." Sadly, teachers of today have identified their major concerns as "drug abuse, alcohol use, pregnancy, teen suicide, rape, robbery, assault, gang warfare, and guns in the classroom." Problems like these can create disruptive environments that threaten children's academic and social success. We believe that we must capitalize on the positive outcomes of change while doing everything possible to eliminate the negative ones. We further believe that maximum learning can take place only when students know how to pay attention and behave themselves *and* want to pay attention and behave themselves. Time To Teach! describes a discipline program that is already fostering maximum learning in diverse classrooms across the country.

Belief #2: Teachers are doing an incredible job.

Contemporary teachers are doing a better job than ever before, even as they face new and greater challenges. We are amazing people who are somehow able and willing to juggle an overwhelming number of tasks and still help kids learn. Not only do we teach; we also parent, nurse, counsel, and lobby for children, to name just a few of the roles from an ever growing list of expectations placed on us. Carolyn Warner's "Litany" is the best list we have seen of some of the roles assigned to teachers over the past half-century.

THE LITANY

Give specialized instruction for the hard of hearing, the blind, the developmentally disabled, the mentally challenged, and the gifted (and be politically correct while doing so); develop special programs for at-risk students; build respect for the worth and dignity of the individual; do eye testing; schedule inoculations; assist bladder control; maintain health records and age certification data; attend faculty department/grade meetings; attend professional workshops; work on an advanced degree; volunteer to supervise extra-curricula activities; participate in fund-raising; collect money to rebuild the Statue of Liberty; stress the prevention of drug, alcohol, and tobacco abuse; promote physical fitness and good nutrition habits; eradicate head lice, scabies and other diseases; inculcate morals, ethics and values; maintain order and teach self-control; provide pregnancy counseling; monitor restrooms, playgrounds, hallways, parking lots, and the cafeteria; discourage food fights; break up fist fights; pray that there are no knife fights; develop individual and civic responsibility; eliminate gender bias and sex discrimination; promote ethnic and racial tolerance; develop an appreciation of other people and other cultures; protect civil rights; help develop political know-how; teach sex education and AIDS prevention; provide suicide counseling; give First Aid instruction; train students in pulmonary-coronary resuscitation; teach the principles of free enterprise; teach management of money, property, and resources; assist in career planning; develop skills for entry into a specific field; teach etiquette and telephone manners; do job placement; serve hot breakfasts and lunches; dispense surplus milk; teach driver training; stress bicycle, automobile, and pedestrian safety; keep up with the latest educational trends and be ready to implement them; know the latest education "buzz" words; assist with bilingual language development; instruct in speed reading; encourage metric education; promote computer literacy; purchase enrichment materials with your own money; counsel students with small problems; counsel students with major problems; protect student privacy; communicate with parents; detect and report child abuse; follow due process procedures; unteach the 4 food groups; teach the pyramid and that broccoli is good; build patriotism and loyalty to the ideals of democracy; instill an understanding of our country's rich heritage; develop the ability to reason; encourage curiosity and a thirst for life-long learning; develop skills in the use of leisure time; promote a feeling of self-worth; teach pride in work; avoid religion; and teach reading, writing, and arithmetic.

Permission to reproduce given by Carolyn Warner, former Arizona Superintendent of Public Instruction

How many of us, upon revealing our profession to a new acquaintance, have heard, "They couldn't pay me enough to do what you do!" (And how many of us have wanted to reply, "They don't pay me enough, either"). When we encounter teacher bashing, we need to remember that most people are in awe of our courage and our abilities. We owe no one any apologies. We are doing an outstanding job under very difficult circumstances. This book describes a program that is helping outstanding teachers do an even better job, helping struggling teachers find their groove, helping new teachers shine, and helping administrators provide a fun, safe and orderly environment for the children of their community…all while having more fun at the same time!

Belief #3: "Kids don't care how much you know until they know how much you care."

Madeline Hunter said it first, and research, personal experience, and common sense all reiterate that students need to feel known, liked, and respected before they can accept instruction. Another way of looking at it is that a classroom with a positive feeling tone is a better learning environment than one that is negative. That's why we present a strong, positive approach to discipline, an approach that allows for mutual respect. That's why our program is about students learning to take personal responsibility rather than about teachers punishing kids. That's why we will be talking about contingent and non-contingent interactions. That's why teachers and students using this program are liking themselves and each other more, even as kids are being held accountable for appropriate behavior.

Belief #4: Good discipline is a matter of good timing.

Just as there are "teachable moments," there are also "correctable moments." We believe that a key to good discipline is timing, and that the time to discipline is very early in the "chain of behavior" – before minor infractions become major ones. This program describes in detail how to achieve good timing consistently and explains why this is important.

Belief #5: Conflict is an essential part of growing up.

Children are designed to pinpoint our weaknesses. That is their job. They are good at it. Expect it. Throughout their school years, students will continually challenge each other and us. This is not to say that they are bad or misguided, but that they naturally seek areas of uncertainty in order to determine the limits within which they must operate. This is a necessary and healthy part of social and intellectual development. In order to maintain our professionalism and sanity, we must remember that "challenging" behavior is only a manifestation of this internal question that all children and young adults ask: "Do you care enough about me to let me know what is right and what is wrong?" Time To Teach! helps teachers provide a predictable environment with clear limits and expectations, consistent and effective discipline, and adequate supervision, while at the same time turning the inevitable and frequent challenges into opportunities for learning – and, incidentally, seeing those challenges decrease in frequency as students "get the message."

Belief #6: Parenting affects behavior.

All teachers know that, for good or bad, what children have learned at home carries over into school. Furthermore, good parenting happens in families of all kinds, in all communities, without regard to race or ethnicity, religion, economic status, or family structure. We see the results of excellent parental guidance in children across all levels of our society, just as we see the results of poor or non-existent parenting across all social levels. We also see many parents who fall somewhere in between expert and incompetent, most of them very sincerely wanting to do better but not always sure how. Under this program, students who have been taught to behave appropriately can enjoy a peaceful academic environment, while the other students are learning – at school – the appropriate behaviors that were not taught at home.

Belief #7: We cannot use poor parenting as an excuse for not teaching.

"God grant me the serenity to accept the things I cannot change and the courage to change the things I can," begins the prayer. We cannot change the way children have been parented (although sometimes we can very positively affect the way they are parented in the future.) Nor can we change biological or psychological factors impacting children's behavior. We certainly cannot discriminate against those children deprived of effective parenting or handicapped by physical or emotional injury. All children deserve the very best education we can deliver. Regardless of the origin of a problem, teachers can do a great deal to help a student be successful. Not only can we enjoy and appreciate the children who have already learned to be respectful, motivated, and responsible, but we can also teach the disrespectful to be respectful, the unmotivated to be motivated, and the irresponsible to be responsible. Teachers using Time To Teach! are doing just that.

Belief #8: Problem behavior can entrap us.

We believe that problem behavior is captivating in nature – in other words, we often cannot resist the temptation to take turns when dealing with intractable students. Typically, problem students exhibit a sequence of behaviors (e.g., off-task – arguing – defiance – physical aggression) that is not only frustrating, escalating, unsafe, and deleterious to academic performance, but also engages us in a very predictable exchange. Engaging in this dynamic is like climbing a set of stairs. The parent or teacher plays an active role by warning, warning again, and warning yet again. Up the stairs they climb, adult and child together, each taking a step in turn, each step more reinforcing for the child, more frustrating for the adult, and less productive for everybody.

Eventually the climbers reach the peak, or the "unbearable limit," which will always be a lose-lose situation for the student, the teacher, and the class. We believe that learning time is too valuable to be spent waiting for teacher and student to reach the top of that staircase. Time To Teach! shows us how to get where we want to go without even starting to climb those stairs, much less reaching the unbearable limit at the top.

Belief #9: Curriculum comes first, but discipline does, too!

An excellent teacher of classroom management wisely advises, "When your discipline falls apart, take a look at your curriculum." If you are losing the whole class, chances are good that they are bored or frustrated or unable to see relevance in their work, and that you need to adjust your unit or lesson plan. The finest disciplinarian in the world is not a teacher without something to teach and the skill to teach it. Among all the tasks that teachers juggle, two are paramount: curriculum and discipline. Neither is more important than the other.

We also assert that neither can be effective without the other. Obviously, sound curriculum is supported by effective discipline. This book is not about curriculum. It assumes that teachers either have mastered their curriculum and their methods of instruction, or are working toward that mastery. There are many fine curriculum resources, but this is not one of them. This book is about how good discipline can promote learning in your classroom, thus giving you more Time To Teach! (True story: after implementing this program in her classroom, one teacher added so much teaching time that she was scrambling to beef up her lesson plans!)

Belief #10: Self-esteem matters.

Current researchers widely accept the premise that self-esteem is significantly associated with personal satisfaction and effective functioning.   Perhaps the greatest combination of studies ever conducted on the antecedents and consequences of self-esteem was produced in 1967 by Stanley Coopersmith of the University of California, Davis. Coopersmith studied the conditions that lead an individual, child or student, to value him or herself. He found that *parental warmth, clearly defined limits,* and *respectful treatment* were clearly the antecedents to high self-esteem. Coopersmith found that young people high in self-esteem were happier and more effective in meeting environmental demands than were persons with low self-esteem. How sad that there has been so little investigation of classroom or school-wide models which cultivate happier and more effective students while holding them accountable for behaving appropriately. . .until now!

Time To Teach! supplies teachers with the appropriate tools for building a classroom with clearly defined limits, mutual respect, and warm emotional support. These are the conditions necessary to foster high self-esteem. Above all, though, our major intent in the Time To Teach! program is to supply children with the building blocks of self-esteem – one of which is taking personal responsibility for one's own behavior. From these building-blocks children can construct social and educational success (e.g., better concentration, better work, better grades, less bickering, less fighting, etc.). Students will find themselves with far more time for learning.

Belief #11: Students do not necessarily know how to behave.

One of the most unchallenged assumptions in schools today is that expected or desirable behaviors are already a part of the student's behavioral repertoire. We do *not* accept the notion that all children know how to behave when they arrive at school. This *is* a faulty assumption, and to accept it is deleterious to youth at large. There are some children who come to school unsocialized and unaware of expectations and who may negatively affect your classroom. It is not our job to judge these students, but it is our job to welcome them and then teach them the school expectations. Yes, we teach expectations at school and – furthermore, after more than three decades we now know that teaching expectations in the first days of school is as important as teaching academics. The results are impressive. At the end of the year, our children have learned more, teachers have taught more, and both are happier.

Various discipline systems are reactive in that they are employed in reaction to student behavior. Once the child behaves in a particular way, the teacher implements the strategy. In Assertive Discipline, negative consequences follow undesirable behavior and positive consequences follow desirable behavior. In Positive Discipline, strong reinforcement is given for appropriate behavior. In problem-solving approaches, occurrences of problem behaviors set the occasion for the students to make better choices about behavior. In general, all approaches have the same intended outcome of increasing pro-social behavior. However, we need a more proactive model to teach students better ways of responding *before* they engage in inappropriate behavior. Time To Teach! is such a model.

Belief #12: Classroom rules and routines need to be systematically taught.

Even the most eager-to-please, well-behaved children imaginable do not know how to act in our classrooms until we have taught expected behaviors. Time To Teach! provides specific methods and strategies for "teaching to" expected behaviors. We give up the first week, and in some schools – weeks – teaching our students from K-12 every behavior they will need in order to be successful in their school setting. Understand that we have traded teaching academics in the first week(s) of school in favor of teaching expectations or behaviors. We have seen again and again the value of time spent at the beginning of the year in truly teaching – not just explaining – expected behaviors. We now teach more and our students learn more. We are happier and our students are happier. Our school buildings are calmer, and our parents are more satisfied.

Belief #13: Teaching succeeds where punishment fails.

It is our conviction that punishment alone does not change behavior over the long term. A student may choose to "behave" in the presence of a punitive teacher in order to avoid a consequence, but what happens when that teacher is no longer present, whether in the classroom or in the student's life? All too often, the student repeats the undesirable behavior in spades, and when student and teacher get involved in a confrontation about punishment, where does it end? Often, the student winds up in the office (or worse), and the teacher in emotional burn-out. We assert that the time to punish needs to be transformed into Time To Teach!

Belief #14: We need an effective consequence for low-level misbehavior.

If punishment does not work, then clearly we need something that does. Time To Teach! includes a simple, respectful, instructional discipline method used successfully in thousands of classrooms across America from grades K-12. REFOCUSING is a shorthand name for the seminal consequence used in the Time To Teach! program. We have seen for ourselves that it is the most powerful solution there is to problem behavior.

Belief #15: An effective discipline program teaches responsible behavior.

We believe that discipline programs promoting anything other than independent behavior in children are doomed for failure. Authoritarian, or heavy handed, approaches lead to resistance and rebellion, and permissive, or wishy-washy, approaches lead to disrespect and chaos in the classroom. Both are doomed to fail. We can no longer subject our children to these "junk science" systems of discipline which have no empirical validation, do not promote self-esteem, do not improve teacher satisfaction, and do not improve academic performance. Time To Teach! methodology is based upon an *authoritative* approach to child management which, in short, means that we will always give our students a choice – and then honor that choice. If our students choose wrong, we will be there for correction. If our students choose right, we will be there for acknowledgement. It *is* that simple.

Belief #16: We can make a difference to every child!

Teachers have amazing power for good in the lives of children. We need to trust our own powers, to hone our already considerable skills, to give proven methods a chance, and to trust in our own abilities to teach and our students' abilities to learn. In the realm of discipline as well as in the realm of academics, truly it is Time To Teach!

CHAPTER 2

TIME TO LEARN FROM GOOD PARENTS

As teachers, we have much to learn from those parents who so successfully prepare their children to behave well in our classrooms. What can effective parents teach us? And how can we apply those lessons to our classrooms? Here are the elements that parents use to teach their children to behave appropriately.

Unconditional positive regard.

Good parents love their children unconditionally. Why? Just because they are theirs. Don't panic! We do not expect teachers to love their students with the same fervor, but we do know that effective teachers are willing to like their students (although not always their behaviors!) and to let them know, by word and deed, that they are liked just because they are members of the class. For parents, this is unconditional love. For teachers, we call it "unconditional positive regard."

Whatever we name it, it is an essential ingredient of a well-disciplined classroom.

Warmth and nurturing.

Loving parents are warm and nurturing. They show their children love and keep them safe. They treat them with respect. Teachers who like their students do the same. They maintain a positive feeling tone, they disallow put-downs, they catch kids doing things right, they model respectful behavior. Certainly, individual teacher personalities come in countless types, from business-as-usual to off-the-wall to tender-and-motherly, but all effective teachers show respect for their students.

Clear expectations.

Effective parents set specific guidelines and limits for their children. "Stay in the yard" is not enough. An effective parent of a preschooler says, "You may be on the grass but you must never step on to the sidewalk or beyond." "Do your homework" is not enough. The wise middle-school parent sets the study time from 3:30-5:30 and the place at the kitchen table. "Be home on time" is not enough. The savvy parent of a teenage driver says, "Have the car in the garage and yourself in the house by midnight." In the same fashion, effective teachers set clear and reasonable guidelines for expected behaviors in the classroom.

One request.

Perhaps the most important characteristic of good parents is that they don't have to "say it twice." In reality, they don't *choose* to say it twice. When the child disobeys, effective parents give one and only one request for compliance. After that, they provide a consequence.

Effective teachers follow the same procedure. They give one request. After that, they provide a consequence.

Consistency.

Raising responsible, happy, and healthy children is not easy. It is hard work. Effective parents do not rely on the "big consequence" to keep their children's behavior in check. They wisely use both positive and negative consequences following good or bad behavior – *every single time.* They never rely on the "magic consequence" to solve problem behavior. Rather, they invest "time" in their children, and care enough to consequent appropriate and inappropriate behavior every time it occurs. Highly skilled teachers follow the same guidelines (probably because they are good parents – first). As Rick travels around the United States presenting at conferences, training in schools, working with school districts, and presenting to parents, he is most often asked this question: "What is the magic consequence…what can I do that will stop that behavior." And the answer is…consistency. It is never the consequence, over the long term, that produces happy, healthy, well behaved children. It is always the level of intensity with which the parent, care giver, or teacher involved himself in the child's life in terms of follow through.

Prompt time-out.

For children of all ages, the most common consequence provided by effective parents is an immediate and relatively short "time-out." The preschooler who inches her foot onto that forbidden sidewalk will find herself back in the house for a while. The middle schooler who skips his afternoon homework time will be back at that table during primetime. The teenager who is five minutes late will not be driving the car next week. Wise parents promptly administer and consistently enforce these time-outs.

Because they expect children to take responsibility for changing their own behavior, parents keep the length of the time-out open. They wait until the child shows readiness to return, even after a very short time, rather than setting a time certain that must be "served." Time out should never be based on an arbitrary number. There are "experts" who suggest a child should stay in time out "one minute for every year old he or she is." Discerning parents will question the "experts" rationale for the "one minute for every year" time-out method. And upon closer inspection, those wise parents have discovered that there is no valid research that would support such a method. It is arbitrary and near sighted, and will not work. Time-out should only, and always, be based upon behavior. To have the child remain in time-out for an arbitrary amount of time borrows theoretically from the authoritarian paradigm – which you will remember leads to resistance and rebellion. Wise parents *allow* reentry from time-out when the child's behavior suggests that he or she is ready to return. The adult is in control, but so is the child. Properly used, time-outs are equally effective for teachers.

No repeated warnings.

Forgive us if we lapse into repeated warnings ourselves as we stress that good parents avoid repeated requests, repeated warnings, repeated threats. We have all been in the uncomfortable position of observing ineffectual parent/child interactions in public places:

"Kevin, put that back!"

{Kevin rebuffs parent}

"Kevin, didn't I tell you to put that back? You know you're not allowed to have those."

{Kevin rebuffs parent}

"Kevin, I've told you twice now to put that back."

"Kevin, what are you supposed to do with that?"

{Kevin ignores parent}

"Kevin, if you don't put that back right now you're going to be very sorry."

"Kevin................."

Potential outcome? Either Kevin gets to keep it, the parent returns it himself, or Kevin gets slapped. In all outcomes, the parent has failed because Kevin still hasn't learned to put forbidden objects back upon request.

What will the effective parent do? After request number one ("Kevin, I need you to put that back"), he will find a way to put the child in a time-out. If possible, one adult family member will continue the shopping while another takes the child back to the car. If alone, the parent will leave the half-filled cart with a checker and return with the child to the car for a period of supervised time-out. Time lost from shopping at that moment will reap huge rewards in the future, when the child will know that the parent's request is serious. Strong teachers, too, provide a timely consequence after one request.

No arguments.

It is part of the job description of children and especially of adolescents to initiate philosophical debates about the rightness or wrongness of the parent's current or past decisions. Smart parents know that such debates are non-productive, and do not take the bait. They know how to say, "I understand how you feel.

Nevertheless, this is how it is (or was). End of discussion." These parents listen respectfully, allow the child her right to her feelings, and terminate the discussion. Good teachers do likewise. Otherwise, they are headed up those stairs leading to the unbearable limit.

Our program for classroom teachers is based on the principles of good parenting. You probably already know these principles. If you are lucky you were raised this way, and if you are a parent, you probably raise your own children this way.

CHAPTER 3

TIME TO LEARN FROM OUR FRUSTRATIONS

Every teacher has been frustrated by the misbehavior of children in the classroom. A mouse in the corner of any teachers' lounge in the country would overhear several accounts per week of very trying encounters with students. Non-teachers rightly ask their teacher friends, "Where do you find the patience?" We see our colleagues burning out because of stress. We begin to worry about ourselves as well.

One definition of insanity is continuing to use the same methods after experience has shown they do not work. For the sake of our own sanity, we need to identify why methods fail, understand how they sabotage us, and eliminate them from our repertoire. Let's take a look at some that may sound familiar:

Neglecting to set clear expectations:

In a perfect world, students would come to us ready and willing to behave perfectly and listen intently so we could impart to them all our wisdom. The planet we inhabit isn't like that, however, and in the beginning our students do not know what we expect of them. When we neglect to give kids clear guidelines about everything from entering the classroom to raising their hands to working in groups to handing in papers, we cannot expect them to do those things "right." How can they if they do not know what our "right" is?

Telling without teaching:

English teachers know that the first rule of good writing is "show, don't tell." Convincing writers must provide vivid detail and adequate supporting evidence. The same rule holds in the classroom. Explaining is not enough; expectations for students must be "taught to." Teachers who have merely explained the rules without engaging the students in the active learning of them will be frustrated by their students' poor performance.

Threats:

Whether empty or real, threats are simply non-productive. An empty threat proves the teacher to be a liar and a wimp – so why run that risk by making the threat in the first place? And a threat carried out is a consequence that could have been used without voicing the threat. In any case, threats create a negative feeling tone and cast the teacher in the role of threatener/punisher. Wise teachers avoid frustration by resisting the temptation to threaten.

Losing it over the little stuff:

Years ago, Judy found herself in the embarrassing position of referring a seventh grader to the vice-principal for repeatedly violating the school's "no gum" rule. Gum chewing is hardly a capital offense – but to Judy it had become overwhelming because the girl had repeatedly defied requests until Judy had completely lost her patience. But imagine how a parent might react if told that her child is in the office for gum chewing. Does the teacher have no control over her class? And imagine the vice principal's view of the teacher's disciplinary competence. Above all, what has the girl learned? We cannot allow ourselves the frustration of "losing it" over repeated minor infractions.

Punishing ourselves along with the kids:

"Aha!" you say, "Judy could have assigned the girl after-school detention!" That is true. But at the same time, she would have been assigning herself to enforce that detention. She would have been whittling away some of her precious planning and one-on-one instructional time to mete out a consequence for a low-level behavior. By the end of the detention, we would have had a frustrated teacher, a sulky seventh grader, and perhaps a frustrated parent. This is not to say that after-school detention has no place as a consequence; it is to say that its frequent use as a punishment for minor infractions is a punishment to the teacher as well as to the child. We need alternatives to the frustrations of teacher-administered detentions.

Repeated warnings, *multiple* requests, and reaching the *unbearable* limit:

Here is a worst-case scenario of a teacher and student climbing the staircase to the unbearable limit. In this case, the student reaches his limit first:

Example 1.
Eight graders have arrived to fifth period. The bell has rung.

Mr. Jones: "Hank, where is your history book?"

Hank: "I forgot it in my locker."

Mr. Jones: "Again? That's the second time this week."

Hank: {No response}

Mr. Jones: "I don't want you to go back to your locker. Use the book on my desk."

Hank: "But my homework is in *my* book. How am I suppose to turn it in?"

Hank: "You'll count it as late if I don't go get it!" {agitated}

Mr. Jones: "That's right."

Hank: "That's %$*#@* up!

Mr. Jones: "That's it. Go to I.S.S *right now*"

Hank: "Make me!"

In another scenario, it could be Mr. Jones who reaches his unbearable limit, perhaps even striking the student.

In an elementary classroom, the exchange could be very different but the outcome the same: student, teacher, or both reaching the limit and doing or saying something regrettable.

Example 2:
Students are in the hallway on the way to a specials class (music). Tyrone is wandering aimlessly.

Ms. Jones: "Ty, would you walk in a straight line please?"

Tyrone: "I will." {continues "zigzagging"}

Ms. Jones: "Look at Beth. Please walk like her."

Tyrone: "She's stupid. I don't want to walk like her."

Students: {Begin to laugh}

Ms. Jones: {Stops line}

Ms. Jones: "Let's go back down the hallway and try it again!"

Students: {groaning}

Tyrone: {Dashes to be in the front of the reversing line}

Ms. Jones: "Stop and come here by me!"

Tyrone: "I'll do it better now"

Ms. Jones: {Continues on, hoping Tyrone will do it right}

No matter what the outcome, such exchanges are non-productive and frustrating to all concerned. They drain teaching energy. They need to be stopped before they begin.

Having our buttons pushed:

Kids know how to push our buttons, and furthermore it is in the nature of growing up to do just that. Here is the one that made Judy cry. Near the end of her first exhausting year of teaching five preps in a tiny rural high school, a popular young man in her senior English class announced, "My father says that everyone knows that the two easiest jobs are a teacher and a preacher!" It was probably lucky for Judy that the remark dissolved her to tears, which saved her from falling into the next and even more frustrating trap of. . .

Arguing:

There is no end to the kind of arguments we can get into with kids if we allow ourselves to take the "debate bait." And there is no end to the frustration we can experience if we do, because these are not winnable arguments. Your logic is no match for your student's emotional load. Furthermore, if you lose, you lose, but if you "win," you also lose, because your youthful opponent has lost face. When invited to debate the merits of your homework system, your discipline plan, your choice of textbooks, your past decisions, your seating arrangements, or anything else – avoid frustration. Respectfully acknowledge the student's right to question authority and possibly even the validity of his points as you politely decline to discuss his issue (which is not to say that you might not give the matter some thought). We need to stay out of arguments.

No-win confrontations:

Far more risky than arguing is all-out confronting. Power struggles can get very ugly very fast. When teacher and student have reached the top of that staircase, that unbearable limit, they are in a confrontation. It is a power struggle in which, just as in arguments, there will be no winners. Furthermore, confrontations are more than frustrating – they can be job-threatening or even life-threatening. We need ways to avoid them.

The Negative Ripple Effect:

It is human nature to sympathize with the underdog, and our students are only human. When they witness any power struggle between teacher and classmate, they are very likely to side with the classmate, even when that classmate is guilty as charged, especially if the classmate appears to be "losing." Never forget that when you "take on" one child, you are really "taking on" him (or her) along with twenty-eight of his classmates. Children are trustworthy. They will support one another, even if you are right. So what might begin as an exchange between teacher and student can quickly become an issue between a teacher and an entire class. Like ripples in a pond, negative energy has disturbed the placid surface of the learning environment and caused monumental frustration. We do not want to start those ripples. They do not vanish at the dry edges of the pond. They reverberate back and forth – over a long period of time. The same holds for your classroom.

Cumbersome bookkeeping systems:

Countless discipline systems require teachers to document student misbehavior. In some systems, the paperwork goes to the office, often in the form of a "referral." In other systems, teachers keep track of how many warnings students have been given, in order to lower the boom at warning #___ (fill in the blank). Some teachers voluntarily document troubling incidents, especially in the case of problem students. The amount of time spent "writing things up" can be immense. How many teachers have despaired, "Dealing with all this discipline leaves me with no time to teach!" And yet common sense (and the school district attorney) tell us that misbehavior needs documentation. We need a way to document incidents in a minimum of teacher time.

Frequent office referrals:

Sometimes students commit very serious offenses in classrooms, usually involving controlled substances, crime, or violence. These are appropriate (and, we hope, rare) times to call for administrative help. Districts do not pay teachers enough to solve those problems alone, nor do responsible administrators expect it. But every time a teacher asks for administrative help because of low-level misbehavior, she is courting frustration for at least three parties: teacher, administrator, and student. Her frustration will come from the fact that she has now given her power to the administrator, and all of her students know it. The administrator's frustration comes from spending valuable time dealing with minor infractions instead of matters of school improvement. The student's frustration is complex, but includes needing to learn appropriate behavior and despairing of ever learning it. The cast of frustrated characters will grow if the parents get involved. It is easy to reach frustration overload very quickly if office referrals are the order of the day. We need to reserve the office for the really big problems.

Wasting everybody's time:

Without time, we cannot teach and kids cannot learn. Interactions like repeated warnings, multiple requests, confrontations, referral writing, and trips to the office waste a huge amount of time for teachers, students, administrators, and sometimes parents. Teachers spend countless hours conferencing and documenting. We neglect our well-behaved students while trying to handle the unruly ones. Administrators spend most of their time with relatively petty matters of classroom discipline. Sometimes parents get involved in matters that they perceive to be better handled in the classroom. Instructional time should go to instruction. We need to minimize the amount of instructional time devoted to discipline.

Our non-teaching friends are in such awe of us because we deal with children who do not always behave themselves. Putting themselves in our shoes, our friends imagine how very frustrating such a situation would be for someone unable to remedy it. Indeed, anyone trying to survive in such a situation, with no hope of improvement, would surely be frustrated to the breaking point. Luckily, we are teachers! We have remedies that do work in situations just like this. Students can learn appropriate behavior. Students can choose appropriate behavior. Teachers can reduce frustration and find Time To Teach!

CHAPTER 4

TIME TO ARRANGE THE ENVIRONMENT

Realtors say that the three most important factors in the resale of a house are location, location, and location. While not the most important factor in a discipline plan, proper "classroom ecology" is the first matter of business in a classroom. Wise teachers place students, furnishings, and decorations to their best advantage. They thoughtfully analyze the placement of everything before school starts and re-evaluate it during the year as needs arise. They try to ensure that every person and every item in a classroom is located so as to decrease the likelihood of interruptions and increase the likelihood that learning will take place. Consider these simple recommendations, many of which are well-known to elementary teachers but not as familiar at the secondary level.

Student Desks.

Aim the students at the intended focal point. There is a reason elementary teachers ask for "eyes forward, please." The direction in which students are gazing is the direction to which they are likeliest to be attending. Energy flows where the eye goes! Capitalize on this by seating students so that all of them are facing the focus of attention, whether that is to be the teacher, each other, or something else. If the teacher is to be the main focus of attention, use theater seating. For group work and labs, they face each other, around tables. Instructional objectives, not tradition or whimsy, should dictate the seating arrangement.

Arrange desks to fit your instructional style. Teacher styles vary widely, encompassing the "sage on the stage," the "guide on the side," and numerous styles in between. No one style is better than another, but everything possible should be done to have the seating arrangements match the delivery style. Typical arrangements include traditional rows, dyads (rows of two), horseshoes, and tables. Use the arrangements that best serve your teaching style and learning objectives.

Be as flexible as your furniture allows. Fortunate teachers are supplied with student desks designed to work in a variety of arrangements – desks that can make traditional rows for test-taking, dyads for large-group instruction, and tables for group work. Whatever the classroom furnishings, seek as high a degree of flexibility as possible in the light of instructional needs.

Identify special seating needs. Numerous circumstances govern seating assignments – most commonly vision, hearing, and attentiveness. One of the most frequently asked questions by parents of inattentive kids is, "Where does he sit?" These are parents who know their children and understand how easily distracted they are. Honor their wisdom. At the first signs of inattentiveness, think about a seating change. Sometimes it can make all the difference for a student.

Juggle proximity to support learning. Whatever the seating arrangement, students will probably be near each other.

Sometimes we can capitalize on that nearness. For example, one very useful variation on the traditional single-row-facing-forward seating arrangement is partner seating, or dyads. This arrangement simultaneously allows students to focus on the teacher, teacher to move among the rows easily, and each student to have a "study buddy." But in this and in all seating arrangements, be alert for non-productive social interactions such as dependency, distraction, victimization, etc. Do not hesitate to separate students who do not support one another's learning, nor to pair up those who do. And respect the occasional "loner" who learns best without a seatmate. The first goal of any seating arrangement must be to support learning.

Know when it is time for a change. Staying in the same seats all year can get tedious, so look for appropriate times to make a new seating chart just for the sake of variety. Some teachers move students after each grading period, a good time to identify and relocate neighbors who undermine one another's learning.

Alas, an occasional class can contain such a challenging mix of students that a teacher can despair of ever finding a workable seating chart. ("I can't put everybody in the front of the room!") But informed persistence can pay off, so put those names on little sticky notes and sit down for a game of "classroom chess."

Field of vision.

Keep visual information points distraction-free. Visual information points are places where concepts are explained: chalkboards, whiteboards, overhead screens, "concept" bulletin boards, etc. Keep these areas free of distractions unrelated to the learning objectives. Analyze decorations such as posters. Do they contribute, or do they distract? That cute poster, student art work, or exemplary student project may belong on a different wall – out of the child's direct field of vision. Do not take them down, but be wise in deciding where to place these items. You do not want to compete with such decorations. Learning is an arduous task, and students may reflexively be drawn from the task at hand to the nice pictures on the wall. Put the odds in your favor by arranging your room so that the instructional area is just that.

Provide an accurate clock in full view. Students deserve to know what time it is, and for many of them, not knowing is a big distraction. If students are to enter punctually and depart considerately, they need to know the time. A fully visible, working timepiece is an essential item in any classroom.

Use the board effectively. Write "daily reminder" material legibly and in a consistent place every day. (Aside: if you expect students to read certain reminders every day, provide a time certain for them to do that.)

Chalk talk at the overhead. The beauty of the overhead projector is that it allows the teacher to face his students as he writes, draws, or displays information. Position your projector on a low table or cart, so as not to block anyone's view. Mount the screen as high as possible, at a logical focal point. Use the overhead whenever connecting with your students is critical to your instruction (until, of course, the bulb burns out at the most important part!). Just as importantly, turn it off to command complete attention – and always when the screen is empty. An empty but illuminated overhead or computer screen is distracting.

Place VCR and/or computerized projectors effectively. All kinds of useful gadgets need to be carefully positioned in our classrooms, in order to be seen when needed without distracting students at other times. It's hard for students to ignore even an animated screensaver, so find ways to turn busy screens off or around.

Minimize necessary distractions. Pencil sharpeners – especially electric ones – are necessary distractions. So are computers. So are certain very attractive adolescents. Locate such wonderful and necessary but highly captivating entities as far away from your visual information points as possible.

Situate learning centers sensibly. Students using centers should have little opportunity to distract those who are not. But don't put them too far away! For liability reasons, centers must be clearly visible to the instructor.

Teacher.

Command center stage. How can you place yourself during direct instruction to decrease interruptions and increase the likelihood that learning will take place? To answer that question, examine the classroom features that are beyond your control. Where are the windows? Where are the entrances and exits? Without unlimited resources or a spouse in the construction business, you can not change these circumstances. It is often easy, however, to make sure that you are not competing with stimuli outside your classroom: don't use the window side of a room to deliver directions or critical content. It is difficult for students to maintain focus on your math presentation if your location affords them the opportunity to look over your shoulder and out the window. Likewise, people enter and exit classrooms.

Parents, visitors, other teachers and students often enter at the least opportune times. Standing near an entrance to deliver critical content increases the likelihood that your instruction will be interrupted and that learning, at least for that moment, will cease. All the world's a stage, but not all of your classroom need be your stage. Play out your instructional dramas in areas of the room farthest from potential distractions.

Put your desk where you really need it. Maybe you particularly need your desk to be a place for conferencing with students individually. Then put it at the students' backs. Do you need a quiet place to grade papers during class, as you occasionally monitor on-task behavior? You should have a traditional front or side of the room location. Is your desk used only before and after school but almost never during instructional time? Why not have it in a faraway corner near a window? In other words, position your desk according to what you know you need. Do you often work at a computer during class, whether alone or as part of large group instruction? If so, be sure to position the keyboard so that you are facing the students as you work.

Time for a Testimonial

Analyzing and revising the ecology of your classroom can yield big results. A Wyoming teacher gives this account of what happened after she rearranged her classroom ecology late in the school year:

"After attending a workshop in Cheyenne with Rick Dahlgren, my first task was to analyze my classroom arrangement and the positioning of students. My fourth grade classroom is a rectangular room with the "front" of the room at the north end where the white board and overhead projector screen are located. The entire west wall consists of windows which look out over the playground. There is a door which leads to the hallway in the northeast corner of the room and a door which leads outside in the southwest corner. The doors have never caused very many problems (if it's noisy in the hallway, I just close the door), but the windows have always been a major problem and a source of irritation. There are three times during the day when the primary grades have recess. During these times my students have been known to stare out the

window, even stand up to watch the primary children as they play right outside our windows!

To decrease the competition for my students' attention I moved the "front" of my classroom to the east wall. The students' desks were rearranged into a U-shape with everyone facing east. I was careful to position students who reacted to one another in a disruptive way far apart. When teaching I usually use the overhead projector, so I moved the screen to the east wall, anchoring it close to the ceiling. Below the screen is a large bulletin board. I chose motivational material (lots of "You can do it!" type of messages) and student artwork to display on this board. The white board on the north wall was mostly used to write the daily schedule and to list upcoming events or reminders. I decided to cover most of it with butcher paper and use it as a bulletin board to display student work, leaving a portion of it to continue writing the daily schedule and reminders.

The results have been amazing. *With the desks arranged in the U-shape, everyone's focal point is the front of the classroom where the instruction is taking place. In the past I usually had the desks arranged in cooperative learning groups, which made it difficult to get children to turn around to watch instruction. Now all the children are facing me, which helps them to stay focused on the instruction. Also, I am no longer competing with the playground. The children have their backs to the windows, so they don't even notice when the primary grades have recess. I will never go back to the old set-up of my classroom. Since I made this change two other teachers have tried this arrangement and are also pleased with the results."*

Time spent analyzing and rearranging people and things in your classroom will be time well spent.

CHAPTER 5

GIVING KIDS THE TIME OF DAY

Good parents are simultaneously loving and firm. Effective classroom discipline is likewise both positive and strong. Madeline Hunter told us that "kids don't care how much you know until they know how much you care." She was right. If you doubt it, recall yourself as both a child and a student. What would your life have been like without love and acceptance from your parents? How would you have done in school if your teachers had never interacted with you as a person? A basic human need is to be cared for and respected for who we are, regardless of our abilities or accomplishments.

We believe that the proper way for teachers to show children how much we care is to simultaneously show them unconditional positive regard and hold them accountable for learning appropriate behavior. This chapter is about showing unconditional positive regard. Don't skip it – in your reading or in your teaching!

Adults interact with children in two very different ways, called contingent and non-contingent interactions. Both are important, and neither should be neglected. Every student, every day, should experience both contingent and non-contingent responses from teachers.

Contingent interaction is acknowledgment of a job well or imperfectly done:

- "Wow! You tied your own shoes today!"
- "Nice left hand margin."
- "Excellent use of supporting details."

or

- "Let's make a "g" together."
- "That's not quite right. Let's try that last division step one more time."
- "Can you narrow that topic even more?"

In these situations, the child must do something, right or wrong, to elicit the response from the teacher. The interaction is contingent on the child's behavior. Contingent interactions are essential to the educational process. Teachers work hard to perfect their skills at contingent interactions in their particular academic areas and grade levels. However, were exchanges like these the only kinds of interactions that a student ever had with a teacher, the student would exist as a "human doing," not a human being. She would never know whether the teacher really cared about her. That need for unconditional positive regard is satisfied through non-contingent interactions.

Non-contingent interaction occurs independently of the child's behavior. It is attention for no particular reason except that the adult or teacher is interested in the child as a human being. The interaction does not depend upon the child or student completing some task, saying the right words, etc.... Non-contingent interactions include communication, interest, and involvement.

communication
- "Tell me how your day is going."
- "How's life?"

interest
- "What is your teddy's name?"
- "How did your game turn out?"

involvement
- "Want to play Chutes and Ladders?"
- "Let's talk about this book you're reading."

Non-contingent interactions signal unconditional positive regard. They are undoubtedly the most important part of any discipline program or relationship (teacher/student, parent/child, husband/wife). They build the foundation for healthy relationships. We are adamant that a strong, positive approach to discipline include plenty of non-contingent as well as contingent interaction. This approach promotes self-esteem and leads children to take responsibility for their own behavior. That is why we need to give every student not only a "good job" or "try again" but also – in our various and unique styles – the "time of day."

CHAPTER 6

TIME TO SET EXPECTATIONS

The first month, first week, and first day of school are critical to classroom management. Good teachers devote a great deal of time during the first few weeks of school to the careful teaching of rules and routines. Instead of telling and posting, they teach and practice classroom routines. After all, school days are made up of routines for doing such things as entering the classroom in the morning, raising hands, listening, and turning in homework as well as rules to govern relationships.

Rationale

In scores of classrooms, Rick and his associates have demonstrated that an instructional approach to classroom management yields positive results, among them more on-task time, accelerated learning, and happier students. Teaching to expectations is vital for several reasons:

1. Rules and routines give students a feeling of security.

Students seek the security that structure provides in the classroom, as well as in the home, because security fulfills a basic psychological need. Successful classroom management provides detailed structure in your classroom from day one. Whereas reactive managers go over rules and routines quickly, proactive managers thoroughly teach their students appropriate behaviors conducive to learning and socialization. In the reactive model, very little time is spent on introductions or teaching rules and routines. In fact, these expectations are sometimes discussed only after repeated misbehavior by students! Hapless students learn the rules and routines primarily through direct or vicarious punishment. In the adult world, such a sequence would be analogous to a policeman writing a new law to cover an infraction for which we were just arrested. If ignorance of the law is no excuse, surely absence of the law is wrong, as well. As teachers, we must devote adequate time to clarifying our expectations. Time thus spent will prove to be invaluable.

2. Rules and routines reinforce the skills that every student must have in order to be a successful learner.

Successful learners know how to co-exist in a classroom politely, how to make the best use of their time, how to listen attentively, how to interact respectfully with classmates and teacher, how to attempt to complete work acceptably. Within this structured framework, creativity and critical thinking skills can flourish. Without these conditions, time will be wasted and some children will victimize others. A structured approach does not seek to create automatons or "teacher clones," it seeks to provide conditions under which all students can reach maximum potential. Chaos – or even pervasive disorder – does not provide those conditions.

3. Rules and routines allow a teacher to be a fair disciplinarian.

We have all heard the cry of, "That's not fair." And, of course, we always resist the temptation to enter a philosophical discussion of justice. However, we must also accept the truth that the fairest situation is the one in which the child knows the rules. Certainly, unforeseen circumstances arise, but if we have done a good job of both establishing and teaching basic principles of behavior, even the most off-the-wall student behavior should be covered. A good example of a basic principle is the oft-used rule, "Respect the rights of others." That rule covers many bases! A student who realizes that her decision to spread rumors about a girlfriend was disrespectful of that person's right to privacy is hard-pressed to cry, "That's not fair!" when asked to make better choices.

IMPLEMENTATION

Below are the essential steps in "teaching to" expected behaviors. Of course you will add your own unique twists, but it is important to include these key elements.

1. Identify areas of need.

Generate a short list of five or fewer basic principles to govern your classroom, and a longer list of procedural routines necessary to the smooth operation of your particular classroom. The basic principles (rules) are the ones to post prominently and refer to often. Both rules and routines arise from your best assessment of where your students are experiencing the most difficulty and how you can help them to succeed.

Easy to say if you are an experienced teacher! If not, your best resource is the experienced, respected colleague in your own building. Chances are he will be flattered to be asked and very willing to share his own classroom rules. If you teach in a team, insist at least on sharing expectations, if not developing a mutual list. A second and often overlooked source of rules is the students themselves. Older ones are probably excruciatingly expert on the subject of appropriate classroom behavior, and even younger ones can propose some excellent "basic principles." Kids of any age appreciate the opportunity to "own" the rules by helping to write them and will favorably reward you with better behavior when you include their voice in rule development. If you have never tried having the students write the rules, you might be surprised to find how very high their expectations can be.

Do not be misled, however. In inviting students to help write classroom rules, teachers cannot give away their powers of final decision-making nor of enforcement. Several years ago, Judy's seventh graders wrote six "umbrella rules," one of which was, "Obey any request from a teacher." Knowing how very literal 12-year-olds can be, and knowing that on rare occasions teachers have been known to make inappropriate requests of kids, Judy herself insisted on revising it to read, "Obey any reasonable request from a teacher." (She did not make a big deal of it or go into any lengthy discussions of child-abuse; she merely pointed out that there are appropriate times to question authority.) In other words, she exerted her power to revise the rules if necessary – and of course, throughout the year she exercised her power to enforce them as well.

2. Devote adequate time to "teaching to" the rules and routines.

We cannot overemphasize the need to spend adequate time teaching these expectations. Research – and the testimonials of teachers who have implemented Time To Teach! across America, Canada and abroad – tell us that by spending several weeks at the beginning of a school year on expected behaviors, before seriously addressing academics, teachers find themselves far ahead of schedule on curriculum later in the year. In other words, when students know exactly how to go about learning, they zoom ahead. Caution: be sure that you have the principal's approval to delay academics! And from the beginning provide enough "schoolwork" to satisfy everybody's needs for getting started.

3. Develop a lesson plan for each classroom "teach to."

A Framework – Essential Items of Each Lesson Plan

Each lesson plan should be only one page long and should communicate the following:

GOALS. Every "teach to" lesson plan should contain *measurable* outcomes. ***If you cannot measure it, you cannot manage it – and shouldn't be teaching it!*** State the expected outcomes for teaching the routine.

RATIONALE. Sharing rationale with your students will help avoid the "Why do we have to do this?" question. State why you want your students to behave in this way or how to use this area.

EXPECTED BEHAVIOR. State how a model student would behave. Be specific in your description.

BEHAVIORS. Identify and demonstrate:
   1) positive,
   2) negative, and
   3) "almost-but-not-quite" behaviors for this rule/routine.

MODELS. Demonstrate all three behaviors. Have students demonstrate and practice the positive behaviors, but **never** allow them to demonstrate and practice negative and "almost-but-not-quite" behaviors. **Practice makes permanent, not perfect.**

What does it look like to do exactly the right thing in this matter (student demonstration)? What does it look like to do this task all wrong (teacher demonstration)? And, what might it look like almost right, but not quite (teacher demonstration)? *(This last step is especially crucial for those students who like to test by putting one toe on the line. "Almost-but-not-quite" examples will head them off at the pass.)*

REVIEWS. Acknowledging that students will misbehave or just plain forget even after being taught a specific behavior, use incidents of misbehavior as opportunities to **re-teach** the behavioral skill.

NEW STUDENTS. Provide opportunities for new students to learn the routines. Perhaps a study buddy or a parent volunteer can explain the procedures to the new classmate. Sometimes, particularly when a new student shows a tendency to disrupt, time spent in a whole-class review of procedures might prove very valuable.

POSITIVE REINFORCEMENT. Needless to say (yet easy to forget!), praise students for doing things right!

An example "teach to" lesson plan for good listening follows:

Teach-To: Listening...

GOALS: Raise hand quietly
  Wait patiently
  Answer quickly

Goals:
State the expected outcomes.

RATIONALE: Instructional time increased
  Decrease frustration (teacher & student)

Rationale:
State why you want your students to behave this way.

EXPECTED LISTENING BEHAVIOR

1. Body facing speaker
2. Eyes on speakers face when she is talking, and/or
3. Eyes on board or screen when speaker is writing
4. Bottom in chair
5. Mouth closed
6. Ask questions! (raise hands first)

Expected Behaviors:
How would a model student behave?

IDENTIFY POSITIVIVE, NEGATIVE, AND "ALMOST-BUT NOT QUITE" EXAMPLES

Positive	*Negative*	*Almost-But-Not-Quite*
Body facing speaker	Body turned away from speaker	Body turned slightly from speaker
Eyes focused on speaker	Eyes focused away from speaker	Eyes occasionally on speaker
Eyes focused on board/screen	Eyes focused away from board/screen	Eyes occasionally on board/screen
Not talking	Talking	Mumbling
Empty Hands	Playing with something	Fidgety hands
Right!	**Wrong**	**Almost**

PROVIDE PRACTICE OPPORTUNITIES...

Model Teacher demonstrates for students (positive, negative and almost-but not quite examples)
Lead   Teacher practices with students (positive examples)
Test   Students demonstrate for teacher (positive examples)
   •Note – never let students practice negative examples. Practice makes permanent, *not* perfect.

WHEN STUDENTS FOLLOW GUIDELINES...

Verbal praise - "Thanks for facing me while I was talking," or "Thanks for sitting quietly during the lesson."

WHEN STUDENTS FORGET GUIDELINES...

Prompt - "I need you to face me when I'm teaching," or "I need quiet hands while I teach."

WHEN STUDENTS ARE NONCOMPLIANT (i.e. student ignores your prompt)

REFOCUS (discussed in detail in Chapter 8)
   What was your behavior?
   What did you want?
   What will you do next time?
   Are you ready to join your class?

PROVIDE REMINDERS AND PRECORRECTION... (for students who often exhibit minor misbehavior)
{Before task begins} "Beth, show me what a good listener looks like and sounds like," and "Can you do those things?"

www.timetoteach.com & *www.goteachergo.com*

CHAPTER 7

TIME TO LEARN FROM EXEMPLARY TEACHERS

The bag of tricks used by successful teachers is fatter than Santa's pack on Christmas Eve. Before we look at consequences for misbehavior (Chapter 8), we need to make sure that our own teacher behaviors draw from that well-filled bag of tricks. Let's take a look at the many ways in which fine teachers increase the probability that learning – and discipline – will occur.

PREVENTION

Of course, effective teachers are constantly forestalling misbehavior through excellent delivery of curriculum, beginning with careful teaching of behaviors. But all experienced teachers know that every classroom includes students who will need "extra help" to learn how to fulfill those behavioral and/or academic expectations. Some of that extra help can deter misbehavior before it begins. A number of such strategies are presented here in the order of increasing effectiveness, and also increasing invasiveness.

The first strategy, planned ignoring, is less intrusive to the student but also less likely to change behavior than the last strategy, academic REFOCUSING.

Planned Ignoring. Planned ignoring means that the student's behaviors are intentionally not noticed. In other words, skilled teachers sometimes deliberately overlook attention-seeking behaviors. This decision is not arrived at lightly, however. First, teachers mentally ask themselves these Classroom Integrity Questions:

> *"Am I able to teach?"*
> *"Are the other students able to learn?"*
> *"Is the student in question able to learn?"*

A teacher who can answer yes to all three questions should always keep teaching. For example, the teacher "does not hear" singing or pencil tapping, as long as she is sure that teaching and learning can continue. She knows that if the student's intent is to drain her teaching energy or provoke a confrontation, she will be walking into a trap by responding to the attention-seeking behaviors. The teacher who reacts has unwittingly accepted the hook, line, and sinker. The fight is now on, and more problems, not fewer, will ensue. Wise teachers don't take the bait when they don't have to!

Obviously, some instances cannot be ignored. Planned ignoring is appropriate only for minor incidents. If a student is in danger of hurting himself, ignoring ceases. The important thing is that teacher energy and effort should be saved for those incidents that deleteriously affect learning in the classroom. Sad to say, violent and disruptive students can provide unlimited opportunities to do battle. A judicious teacher makes sure to be the one who chooses that battle.

Signal Interference. Especially in the lower grades, teachers use a variety of signals with their students on a daily basis. Turning the lights off and then on means "I need you with me." The teacher's hand held high means "Pay attention to me now." At the secondary level, students know to get quiet when a teacher moves to the front of the room or an assembly speaker steps to the microphone. Numerous non-verbal cues are used in large group instruction. Similarly, teachers often communicate with individual students non-verbally. They might use a frown or a thumbs down signal to convey dissatisfaction with a student's behavior. Because these signals are nonverbal, they tend not to put the student in an embarrassing position in front of the rest of the class. However, teachers cannot assume that students can "read" their facial expressions or hand signals. When a student fails to respond, it is best to meet privately in order to mutually determine a signal that will cue him or her to stop any behavior which is beginning to interfere with learning. An effective private signal is one which will capture the student's attention. Therefore, it needs to be a signal that is unique and seldom used. A vague signal would be "a hand gesture," whereas a specific and far better signal would be "a hand gesture with all five fingers extended and the wrist bent at 80-90 degrees." Teachers should avoid using signals that are typical parts of their daily behavior (for example, throat-clearing), as the student will think she is doing something wrong every time the teacher unwittingly clears his throat.

Proximity Control. Moving the teacher physically closer to students tends to decrease inappropriate behavior and increase attention. Proximity tells the student that the teacher is interested, engaged, and concerned. During direct instruction, a teacher can move near an inattentive student and instantly regain that focus. Some teachers keep an empty desk near theirs for use on an as-needed basis. In this manner, the desk does not represent a seat for "the bad kid," but is recognized as a working place for any child who needs a little help in concentrating. Proximity control can be used in combination with signal interference, allowing a student to sit closer to the teacher so that the teacher can provide less obtrusive signals. Both strategies help the student to focus attention on the appropriate activity.

Interest Boosting. It is a challenge to maintain the interest of contemporary students. Expert teachers, who know that distracting a student with something of interest may prevent a costly outburst, always have available a few activities of interest to be used if needed. Of course, evaluating the integrity of the classroom is critical in deciding whether to interrupt this student's progress in order to maintain a calm and focused environment; teachers move into interest-boosting only when convinced that learning cannot go forward without such intervention.

A simple and direct form of interest-boosting is to become involved in the lesson on which the student is currently working. Sitting down next to him and working on the assignment together often helps avert non-compliant and self-indulgent behavior. Also helpful are interesting and unusual facts that can be used during various academic lessons (brain teasers, facts from the Guinness Book of World Records, etc.). Most teachers try to determine areas of interest of all of their students and are ready to plug them in as minor modification of lessons. Occasionally, smart teachers are willing to take a complete break from academic rigor for the sake of everyone's returning refreshed.

Use of Humor. Students with problem behavior typically exhibit a sequence of off-task behaviors (e.g., arguing – defiance – physical aggression) that are not only escalating, unsafe, and limiting to academic performance, but also occur together in a very predictable, escalating, sequential manner. This sequence of negative events can be interrupted through the use of humor.

We know that laughter produces physical and emotional relaxation. The classroom teacher can use humor to defuse potentially volatile situations and help the classmates involved feel less threatened and more comfortable. To confront aggression with humor (but never sarcasm) is to send a very powerful message: "I know you are angry, but I am not." The message is intended not only for the unruly student, but also for all of the other children in the classroom. *Remaining calm yet witty is the best gift teachers can give themselves in a time of crisis.*

Support from Routine. The most important thing teachers do for students with behavioral problems is to provide a well-defined, predictable, nurturing environment. Predictability and structure, under the supervision of a caring teacher, are the critical building blocks to healthy development – social, cognitive, and academic. Many teachers involve their students in the development of classroom routines. Much of the current research on student voice indicates that those programs which solicit student feedback are far more successful than those that do not.

Removing Distractions. Distractions can be provided by both students and teachers! Students may bring with them any number of high appeal items marketed for children and adolescents in fierce competition with the teacher. Toy cars, transformers, cassette players, nerfs, and many other items cause distractions and fights among students. Remember pogs? Or trolls? Or giga-pets? Seasoned teachers know that distracters need to be "checked-in" at the door and "checked-out" for the recess or lunchtime. They know to forbid note writing during class. They know that activities like paper-tearing and paper-folding are permitted only when part of a learning activity. Teachers are good at removing student-created distractions – but sometimes all too guilty of providing distractions themselves! Teachers can unwittingly provide all kinds of distracters, ranging from unusual articles of clothing to attention-getting posters to re-arrangement of furniture. Sensitive teachers take a daily look around their classroom from the perspective of a distractible youngster and remove the "neon signs" that can sabotage a great lesson plan.

Hurdle Help. An ounce of prevention is worth a pound of cure. Teachers know this proverb holds true in the classroom. Hurdle help is a timely comment, statement, or gesture at the onset of an inappropriate behavior which helps the student to follow the correct course of action. For example, a high school student who has just crumpled a piece of paper and raised his or her arm to "shoot" it is seen by the teacher, who reminds the student to walk to the trash can to throw it away. It is important to intervene before the misbehavior occurs. A little preventive maintenance can eliminate the need for major repairs later. The teacher should try to provide immediate instruction at the very moment the student initiates the event.

Direct Appeal To Values. *Appeal to values* speaks to a student's interests and is usually experienced as helpful and supportive. It can clarify for students how to behave in ways that are important to them, as well as their classmates. Teachers who do not understand well what their students really value, however, are less apt to strike the right nerve with their appeals. Students with different values or cultural frames of reference may see an appeal to values as teacher hokum. Be sincere and know your students well. They will appreciate it, and they will appreciate you.

Specifically, when a teacher directly appeals to a student's values, the student is encouraged to make a decision as to whether his or her behavior is positively or negatively affecting the learning tone within the classroom. One-on-one conferencing is suggested to promote an understanding of how the students behavior may be making matters worse, and to discover alternate behaviors that can help the student focus attention on the problem at hand and his or her part in it.

Directly appealing to student values is a component of the REFOCUSING process described in Chapter 9. We use a very powerful questioning format which requires "positive" affirmations and mix that with phrasing in our questions that require more involved and higher level thinking, and also ownership in ones behavior (e.g., What exactly were you doing? What did you want (be specific)? What are you going to do next time?). Finally, we seek a commitment for changing a behavior next time the problem occurs.

Distraction. Great teachers routinely draw upon a set of acting skills which allow them, at times, to "put instruction on" in an overly energetic, outgoing, effusive, exuberant, or even morose, melancholic, or pensive manner – all in the name of "gaming" and keeping student attention. The great ones use these skills to teach well, and *also* to divert attention away from certain hot spots, or potential problem areas.

Distraction is similar to hurdle help, especially in the sense that timing is everything. When confrontation or negative behavior is beginning to create a disturbance, focusing the class' attention and/or the student's attention on something different can reduce or eliminate the problem. For example, a student who is verbally challenging a teacher (e.g., "Why do we have to do this?" or "Mr. Smith never made us do it this way!") may stop to listen if the teacher begins "enthusiastically" discussing a topic of interest to the student (e.g., what's for lunch, special events coming up), or if the teacher "exuberantly" begins an activity with the other students he or she knows that the misbehaving student would enjoy.

This "mental" distraction provides opportunity for the student to give up the negative behavior without him or her knowing they have done so. Voila!

Infusion With Affection. Everybody needs to be heard and understood. Students are not an exception to this rule. Positive, supportive, or appreciative teachers help students to respond more appropriately. Psychologists have long understood warm, open, caring responses help others to talk about the problems they are experiencing before the problems build into a significant incident. The same holds true for your students. Try saying "I think you probably feel very sad now, and that makes me feel sad, too." You might follow that up with, "Do you think we might talk about your feelings when I get a chance?"

Interpretation As Interference. This reactive technique is very similar to distraction. Indeed, it is a *way* to distract. Sometimes kids act first, and think next. This is normal. Your student may not understand or be aware of a behavior that is occurring (acting, not thinking). You may find it helpful to describe to the student what he or she is doing by commenting on observable behavior. This serves as a reminder and as a prompt that the behavior is interfering with academics. For example, "When you answer without raising your hand first, it is hard for the others to have a chance, too."

Role-modeling. The most powerful management tool available to teachers is conducting themselves in the manner in which the students are expected to behave. Teachers who display self-control, respect for their students, good manners, and courtesy, honesty, fairness, and good judgment, **teach by example**. Specifically, strive to create a warm, safe classroom climate, provide plenty of feedback, respect individuality and personal integrity, be flexible and fair – firm when needed – and welcome creativity and imagination.

Our students learn by watching us closely and by listening to every word we utter, by noticing subtle mannerisms, body language, and the tone, volume and cadence we use when delivering instruction. Children who regularly challenge often attend to the emotional tone of the teacher with more concentration than actual words. Be a good role-model and have model students!

Antiseptic Bouncing. At times a student should be removed from class or other school activities, yet the situation does not call for a disciplinary intervention. When pressure is building, and we stress the keyword "building," despite the best efforts of teacher and student, the student's absence may be necessary to maintain a positive climate and focused classroom. The intent here is not confrontation, but rather stabilization. In such a case the student can be sent from the room to a) deliver a note to another teacher, prearranged between teachers, b) take something to the office, c) get a drink of water, d) go to the restroom, e) do a simple chore for the teacher. etc.

This procedure, called antiseptic bouncing, has been judiciously used by teachers for more than one-hundred years, but should be relied upon rarely and also must never be seen as a reward for misbehavior. Furthermore, it is imperative that students travel to settings in which neither frustrating nor positive interactions will take place. Students who are already frustrated or angry are never bounced, but students who are beginning to show these signs are bounced early, to help them avoid becoming frustrated and angry. Timing is everything. And so is an understanding of the emotional state of your students before you use this highly useful strategy.

The bounce is used to give the student a break from pressure, not a chance for interaction. Positive interaction spoils the integrity of the intervention and encourages future misbehavior. Students should have been pre-taught the expectations for the environment to which they are moving and should be adequately supervised in that environment. Used only with great caution, antiseptic bouncing is sometimes the perfect way to help a kid "let off some steam."

We said earlier that REFOCUSING is a shorthand name for the seminal consequence used in the Time To Teach! program. In point of fact, REFOCUSING is a powerful refinement of the century old "bounce" strategy, which affects powerful, dramatic, and positive impact on the contemporary classroom. You will learn a great deal more about REFOCUSING, how it is similar to the "bounce" and also how it is different, in Chapter 9.

Prompting. Despite our brilliant strategizing, students do get off-task. Teachers invite students to return to task in many ways.

Verbal prompts are very common and include (in ascending order of effectiveness) questions ("Jack, do you think you can stop tapping your pencil?"), statements ("Jack, I need quiet hands, please."), and directions designed to initiate behavioral momentum ("Jack, you only have to complete the problems which I have circled in red.") Although effective with relatively compliant students, verbal prompts are the least effective of all possible prompts for "needy" kids.

Gestures used as signals – for example, a tapping gesture accompanied by a side-to-side shake of the head – are more effective and less disruptive than spoken requests.

Modeling is often what a reluctant learner needs as a jump-start. After receiving from the teacher a demonstration of how to proceed (for example, completing a couple of math problems with the student), Jack may be off and running.

Moving student into the "learning position" is extremely effective strategy with young "refuseniks." Teachers use this when a student's body language (slouched back in seat, legs stretched out under desk, etc.) proclaims, "This is how I sit when I am choosing not to learn." The teacher's strategy is to guide the student through a part of the learning activity while gently repositioning him ("Jack, I love the way you've begun to work on the math problems." (Teacher gently places Jack's pencil in his hand, straightens Jack's back, and moves Jack's chair closer to the desk top.) Suddenly a surprised Jack finds himself in the physical position that says, "This is how I sit when I am choosing to learn!" Jack's chances of learning have just improved immensely.

Initiating Behavioral Momentum. Rick calls this "The Big Mo" because it is so powerful. Teachers are using behavioral momentum when they assign one or more activities that their frustrated student likes to do (watering plants, handing out papers, sorting, delivering a note, etc.). Odds are that the momentum established when doing these desirable tasks will transfer to traditional learning tasks.

Calm Communication Style. Great teachers call upon a variety of dramatic and interest-getting delivery styles as they impart academic information to students, and our advice is in no way meant to put a damper on those wonderful speaking styles. The context here is the "disciplinary moment" – those times when teachers need either to prompt a student(s) about appropriate behavior or to consequent misbehavior. In these instances, wise instructors temporarily drop the drama and move into a mode best described as business-as-usual. Knowing that calm is contagious, they remain calm both verbally and non-verbally.

Verbally, effective teachers control their tone, volume, and cadence. Their tone is matter-of-fact and free of impatience, condescension, and inattention. They keep their volume appropriate for the distance and situation, neither whispering nor shouting. They deliver their message in a moderately paced cadence or rhythm. Everything about their verbal delivery is low-key and businesslike.

Physically, these teachers control their body language as well. If necessary to approach the student, they do so slowly, taking a supportive rather than a challenging stance. For example, the teacher may choose to stand beside the student rather than face-to-face. Respectful of the student's personal space, they leave at least 1½ - 3 feet between themselves and the student. At all times, the teacher avoids challenge and confrontation. Needless to say, the teacher does not touch the student during a disciplinary interaction!

REMEDIATION

Academic REFOCUSING. Responsible teachers constantly monitor student performance, always on the lookout for areas of confusion or difficulty. When they encounter "academic error" they stop the student, re-teach, check for understanding, and eventually send the student back to work independently. Consider the following academic example:

$$\begin{array}{r} 26 \\ +\ 37 \\ \hline 513 \end{array}$$

In the math problem above, Megan has made a common mistake for a second-grader learning addition with regrouping. Smiling brightly, she approaches Mr. Stone's desk to show him her work. If Mr. Stone were to glance at her work, smile, and say, "No, that's not right, Megan. Go back to your seat and try again," he would be derelict in his duty. Instead, he begins remedial action.

STOP THE LEARNER
If an error has occurred, the first remedial step of effective instruction is to stop the learner. Without re-teaching, the probability is high that Megan will continue practicing the same mistake. It is critical at this juncture that misunderstanding cease. Mr. Stone's appropriate response might be, "No, that's not quite right, Megan. Let's try that problem together."

RE-TEACH THE LEARNER
The second remedial step of effective instruction is to re-teach the learner. Mr. Stone would re-teach Megan the concept of regrouping. Corrective procedures are essential at this point because they allow the student to BEGIN AGAIN without practicing mistakes.

EXAMINE THE LEARNER'S WORK
The third remedial step of effective instruction is to examine the learner's work. After re-teaching the concept, Mr. Stone would have Megan attempt another problem and then check for accuracy.

LET THE LEARNER GO
The fourth remedial step of effective instruction is to let the learner work independently when they have mastered the concept. When Megan demonstrates that re-teaching has been successful, she is encouraged to keep working independently.

These remedial steps, routinely followed in academic settings, are the heart and soul of effective teaching. We are convinced that the same steps are the heart and soul of effective disciplining. Chapter 8 describes how REFOCUSING can be used as a disciplinary tool.

CHAPTER 8

TIME TO DISCIPLINE

In Chapters 1-7 we have reviewed time-honored classroom practices employed by successful teachers everywhere. We have recommended paying careful attention to the classroom environment, to non-contingent interactions, to the systematic teaching of expected behaviors, and to a variety of strategies designed to prevent misbehavior. These practices are presented not as new and revolutionary ideas but as the necessary components of any sound educational program. Knowing that many of our readers already use these practices expertly every day, we nevertheless felt it essential to identify and describe the methods for those teachers not yet familiar with them. We hope that this review has had value for all our readers. **We cannot stress strongly enough that the discipline program described herein cannot succeed unless we first interact positively with our students and systematically teach our expected behaviors.**

So let us assume that these things are in place. Whether school has been in session for one day, one month, or one semester, teachers and students are interacting both non-contingently and contingently, and at least some expectations are being systematically taught. If it is early in the year, there are more expectations to come! It is now time for the students to learn about what happens if they disregard those expectations. Before that lesson can be presented, the teacher needs to understand the process, make some decisions, and lay some groundwork.

The Process: REFOCUSING

REFOCUSING is a discipline plan modeled after the academic remediation model seen at the end of Chapter 7, in which the teacher stops the student, re-teaches, checks for understanding, and sends her back to work independently. Because every classroom situation is unique, the REFOCUSING process is very flexible, allowing for varying designs within its broad framework. However, one of the most common and effective designs involves a "buddy teacher" in another classroom, preferably not very far away. When working with a teacher/partner is impractical, impossible, or inappropriate to the situation, the teacher manages all steps of the process within the classroom. The two arrangements are referred to as buddyREFOCUS® (in partnership with one or more colleagues) or soloREFOCUS® (all in one room).

By "making decisions" we mean that teachers considering this discipline program will need to design it to fit their situation. By "laying groundwork," we mean that a teacher who decides to use the buddy system will need to recruit a nearby colleague to be that buddy. Do not be misled. The colleague need not be personally committed to this program for her own classroom (although that would be great), but must be willing to help you pilot it in your own classroom by being willing to REFOCUS your students in her classroom. She may be motivated to participate by curiosity about how the program works, or just by a desire to be helpful. Whatever the motivation, treasure your friend's willingness to work with you and respect his right to understand, question, or even (but we hope not) rebel.

We have previously established that there are some similarities between ineffective family management practices and our traditional approach to problem behavior in the classroom. In particular, traditional responses to problem behavior in classrooms, like ineffective family management practices, consist of repeated warnings and multiple requests. During one of Rick's workshops, one teacher summed it up perfectly. She said, "We have been conditioned, in fact taught in college, to give kids lots of chances." From an academic perspective, we believe that students deserve "lots of chances," that they should be given a wide variety of academic choice and the opportunity to meet, and sometimes fail, academic challenge. **From a discipline standpoint, we believe that it is not the time for "lots of chances" when a student demonstrates inappropriate behavior. It is the time for quiet, quick guidance.** It is an opportunity to learn from a mistake. We believe that we must not let misbehavior pass by, because to do so is to reveal to the student that we either do not care enough or do not have enough time to let him know what it was that was causing difficulty or interfering with learning.

In dealing with problem behavior (an abstract, general concept), we focus on the treatment of student noncompliance (a specific, describable event). We have identified three critical elements for an effective approach to classroom management. First is to replace warnings and/or repeated requests with early intervention. This is critical because a behavioral chain is weakest at its beginning. The second element is contingent withdrawal of attention when a problem behavior occurs: a time-out. The final element is a combination of procedures intended to achieve self-directed behavior and behavioral momentum (sequence of high probability compliance-command events). Our shorthand term for this entire process, from intervention through time-out to self-directed behavior, is REFOCUSING.

Across America, Canada, and abroad teachers, schools, and districts trained by Rick Dahlgren are using this program in elementary, middle and high schools serving large numbers of students at risk for school failure. The results are impressive. Teachers have demonstrated its effectiveness in classrooms, pods, teams, grade levels, schools, and entire school districts. At the building level we have seen a dramatic decrease in disciplinary actions (e.g., suspensions, office referrals). At the classroom level students are not only demonstrating more on-task behavior, but teachers report more energy for instructional activities. Finally, the program has succeeded with a wide range of children. This is not to say we have "cured" them all. Rather, we are making steady progress with children who previously saw little success in school, and teachers are better able to focus on the teaching and learning process.

In order to more fully understand this process, we will illustrate each step as it would occur in our schools.

This intervention can happen within a single classroom
    (**solo**REFOCUS)
or between two or more teachers (very powerful)
    (**buddy**REFOCUS).

1. Early Intervention

It is critical that teachers respond early in the behavioral chain. We have found that this notion is difficult for teachers to accept because they have learned (in some cases have been asked) to tolerate a high level of annoying and unproductive behavior. It is also critical that threats and ultimatums, as well as warnings, be eliminated. *The interaction should be matter of fact and unemotional.* We recommend simply giving the student a start-up request (e.g., "I need your attention here").

2. Prompting

Prompting is the most important step in preventing low-level behavior from becoming serious, challenging behavior. If a student misbehaves, it is imperative that he or she be given a prompt, which is a request for changed behavior. Close attention must be paid to how and when the prompt is given.

Framing the prompt as a start-up request. It is important to see the advantage of start-up over shut-down requests, which have the same intended outcome (to change student behavior) but are far less effective. To help illustrate the difference, consider the following:

John, a fourth-grader, is tapping his pencil on his desk while Mr. Jones is teaching.

> **Start-up request***:* "John, I need quiet hands, please."
>
> **Shut-down request***:* "John, stop that."

Both requests are delivered in a matter-of-fact, nonjudgmental tone; both are succinct and clear. In many ways they are very similar, yet they remain deceptively different. A shut-down request signals the student to terminate behavior, (i.e., *"Stop that"*) and suspends positive behavioral momentum (the probability that the student will continue responding appropriately). A start-up request, on the other hand, signals the student to initiate an appropriate replacement behavior (i.e., I need quiet hands please") and accelerates positive behavioral momentum. Moreover, from a child's perspective, a shut-down request is likely to be understood as *"Quit it,"* and a start-up request as *"Try it."* Replacing shut-down requests with start-up requests has a profound and positive impact on both teacher and students.

3. Timing the prompt

Teachers often ask, "When should I prompt?" We always suggest asking the three classroom integrity questions before prompting:

> *"Am I able to teach?"*
> *"Are the other students able to learn?"*
> *"Is the student able to learn?"*

Recall the example we previously used:

John, a fourth-grader, is tapping his pencil on his desk while Mr. Jones is teaching. If Mr. Jones can answer yes to all three questions, he continues with instruction. He may hear John tapping his pencil, but if he can still teach and if the other students can still learn (i.e., the tapping is not interfering with their learning) and if John can still learn, the academic integrity of the classroom has been preserved. Mr. Jones does not intervene. We believe that teaching energy is too valuable to drain on one student, especially when twenty-five or more students are still "with you" and able to learn.

On the other hand, Mr. Jones may not be able to answer yes to all three questions. For example, the tapping may be interfering with the other learners. If he cannot answer **yes to all three questions**, he should prompt the student with a start-up request.

Start-up request:
"John, I need quiet hands please."

If the tapping stops, Mr. Jones should positively reinforce the student. A myriad of positive acknowledgments may be used depending on the age of the student (i.e., thumbs up, wink, private/public "thank-you," etc.).

4. Graceful Exit

If the tapping continues after prompting, Mr. Jones is faced with a more serious challenge of noncompliance, a challenge which must not be ignored. Mr. Jones must respond, not from a need to control or punish the student, but from a desire to inform the student about what it is that is interfering with his academic learning or social conduct.

SoloREFOCUS: The response is to direct the noncompliant student to a designated spot in his own classroom if Mr. Jones is using soloREFOCUS, or...

BuddyREFOCUS: to a "buddy" teacher's classroom for REFOCUS if he is using buddyREFOCUS.

Mr. Jones will give his directions in whatever manner has been previously taught, or in other words will deliver a clear and concise statement for the student to begin REFOCUSING. It may be a simple gesture toward the doorway (buddyREFOCUS), or a table in the back of the room (soloREFOCUS), or it may be a brief direction like, "REFOCUS please" (a directive used to initiate either buddy or soloREFOCUS).

The student moves to a previously established area of the classroom to get a REFOCUS form and takes it to the back of the classroom to the REFOCUS area (soloREFOCUS), or takes it to the buddy teacher/partner's classroom (buddyREFOCUS).

Note: We suggest that kindergartners: a) always REFOCUS verbally and, b) never leave their own classroom.

5. Graceful Entrance

SoloREFOCUS: The student should quickly move to the designated REFOCUS spot in his or her own classroom, complete the form and put down his or her pencil when finished. When observed sitting in a calm manner, the classroom teacher approaches the student, or summons (gestures) the student to approach with the REFOCUS form. **The classroom teacher checks the form for accuracy.** Timing must be favorable for the classroom teacher and also the teaching process. The classroom teacher should always meet with the student when a natural break occurs during instruction and never during important teaching moments.

BuddyREFOCUS: The student should quickly go to the "buddy" classroom. As a matter of courtesy, the student should stand in the doorway of the designated buddy classroom and wait until the buddy teacher directs him or her to the REFOCUS area (e.g., a desk in the back of the room). Recognition of the student is at the convenience of the buddy teacher, and should be done at a time that is least disruptive to the second class. The student should quickly move to the designated REFOCUS spot in the buddy room, complete the form and put down his or her pencil when finished. When observed sitting in a calm manner, the buddy teacher approaches the student, or summons (gestures) the student to approach with the REFOCUS form. **The buddy teacher checks the form for completeness, instead of accuracy.** The classroom teacher will check for accuracy when the REFOCUSING student returns to his or her homeroom. Timing must be favorable for the buddy teacher and also the teaching process. The buddy teacher should always meet with the student when a natural break occurs during instruction and never during important teaching moments.

Best Practice: Buddy teachers' classrooms should be near one another.

Note: A buddy teacher does not problem solve, encourage, engage, support, or help the REFOCUSING student. A buddy teacher only provides the REFOCUSING student a neutral setting to independently think about his or her behavior and determine a more productive course of action upon returning to class. Correctly discharging his or her duties, the buddy teacher will notice little to no impact on his or her classroom and teaching time during the REFOCUS process.

6. REFOCUS Form

REFOCUS requires the students to answer the following questions in sequential steps: a) What was your behavior? b) What did you want? (e.g., revenge, attention, to not do the homework, etc.) c) What should you have done instead? and d) What do you plan to do in the future? Some sample REFOCUS forms are located in the back of this handbook. It is important to note that some teachers may use different questions. However, we recommend that teachers always ask students what they did and what they will do next time.

The student can be either verbally REFOCUSED (i.e., the teacher asks him or her the questions), or can answer the questions on the REFOCUS form in writing. If the student is agitated, the teacher responds by saying "I'll be back to you" and returns to teaching until another natural break arrives (and until the student is sitting in a calm manner). This step may need to be repeated. Throughout this process the teacher does not cajole or get drawn into a discussion with the student. The interaction should be matter-of-fact and nonjudgmental. The implicit message is, "I care enough about you to help you identify what it was that was interfering with your academic learning or social conduct." The explicit message is, "The primary agenda in our classroom is learning, not misbehaving."

7. From defiance to enlightenment

After the student has finished REFOCUSING, either verbally or in writing, he waits for the teacher to check to see that the answers on the REFOCUS form are acceptably written and accurate (solo) or acceptably written and *likely* to be accurate (buddy). The teacher directs the student to return to his or her spot in the classroom (soloREFOCUS) or to his or her own classroom with the completed form (buddyREFOCUS).

"But," you may be wondering, "What if the student is unable to identify the behavior which was interfering with his or her learning?" This is a common question with a very encouraging answer. Among the tens of thousands of students who are learning in classrooms using this discipline method, we have never encountered one student who was unable to identify the behavior which was impacting their learning. The reason is that we put such great emphasis on the importance of prompting. Recall that if a student is misbehaving or disrupting the class, the teacher thinks through the three classroom integrity questions:

> *"Am I able to teach?"*
> *"Are the other students able to learn?"*
> *"Is the student able to learn?"*

If the teacher is unable to answer yes to all three questions, she prompts the student in the form of a start-up request. (Start-up request: "John, I need quiet hands please.") In this fashion, we are prompting the student to help him or her identify the behavior which is beginning to interfere with learning or social conduct.

The prompt is a catalyst which targets, identifies, and defines a solution for the student exhibiting emergent misbehavior. He or she is now aware. This illustrates why our students are never unaware of their misbehavior when REFOCUSING. They have been given a fair chance. They have failed. We believe their failure presents an opportunity to help them identify positive solutions which will lead to success the next time around!

Without the use of prompts, Time To Teach! could be mistaken for one of many so-called "zero-tolerance" programs for misbehavior. In our opinion, such approaches are unsuitable for children and students and negatively impact their social, emotional and academic well-being. If you don't use prompts, don't use this program. Period.

8. Check for understanding.

The answers, whether spoken or written on the REFOCUS form, must be accurate (i.e., the student must correctly identify the behavior which was interfering with his or her learning or social conduct). If incorrect, the student is directed to return to the designated spot for REFOCUS. Throughout this process neither the teacher (soloREFOCUS) nor the buddy teacher (buddyREFOCUS) is drawn into a discussion with the student. All interaction should be matter of fact and nonjudgmental. There is no set time limit on when the teacher should have the student answer the questions on the REFOCUS form. The time required for the intervention is dependent upon the student (how long it takes him or her to become calm and responsive to positive adult-student interactions) and upon both the homeroom teacher and the buddy teacher (waiting for an appropriate moment when interacting with the misbehaving student will be least disruptive to the rest of the class).

9. Welcome Back.

When the student is ready to re-enter the home classroom (buddyREFOCUS) or go back to the seat (soloREFOCUS), he should wait to be acknowledged by the teacher. Waiting to be acknowledged is an expected act of courtesy and respect on the part of the student; it is not about a need for control on the part of the teacher. When time permits, the teacher will approach the student. In a positive but matter-of-fact manner, the teacher will direct him to rejoin the class. It is critical that the student is welcomed back in a businesslike, nonjudgmental tone. Too warm a welcome ("I'm SO glad you are back in class. . .are YOU glad to be back in class?") will reinforce misbehavior and send a mixed message to the student. Indeed, he may be willing to misbehave in the future to get this kind of attention from you. Too negative a greeting ("Well, are you going to try and work now?") is demeaning and may spark another challenging episode. We suggest using an affirmative response (i.e., "It's good you're back; we're working on math") which is intended to let the student know that she is indeed welcome back, that she has a clean slate, and that learning is the primary agenda in your classroom. An appropriate welcome will signal neither too much nor too little.

USE OF OTHER CONSEQUENCES

REFOCUS is a proven and powerful response to most low-level problem behavior, but it is by no means the only allowable or suitable response. It can and should be used flexibly with other school and classroom strategies and consequences. For students exhibiting chronic problem behavior, we recommend that, while continuing to use REFOCUS, teachers or administrators feel free to develop additional contingencies. What teachers find remarkable, however, is how seldom those chronic misbehaviors emerge under this system. As teachers take time to discipline by this simple, yet powerful and respectful program, they begin to enjoy far more Time To Teach!

CHAPTER 9

TIME TO REFOCUS

You may have arrived at this program by any one of a number of paths. Perhaps after reading this book, you decided to pilot it in your classroom. You or a colleague may have taken a Time To Teach! workshop. Maybe a colleague has asked you to buddy up for a test run. Possibly an enthusiastic administrator has suggested the program to you. (We hope it has not been mandated, but we are aware that mandates sometimes happen.) However you got here, we encourage you to give this program adequate time. Like most things in life, this system is a process. Like most good things in life, it will sell itself over time. And like most effective things in life, it takes time to prove itself – although we think you will be surprised to see some very positive results almost instantly. We recommend that you follow these steps as you prepare to implement Time To Teach! in your classroom:

First, give yourself plenty of time to understand the necessary components of the program. Go over the checklist (page 118). Review concepts if necessary. When you think you know where you're headed, explain it to another teacher. Is it making sense? In your gut do you feel it might work for you? Are you willing to cover the necessary bases? Have you enlisted support from colleagues or administrator? Don't attempt to implement the program until you feel comfortable with it.

Second, and so very important, teach to your behavioral expectations. Please don't tell and post. If you are already into the school year, review and re-teach what was covered earlier, perhaps clarifying problem areas.

Third, teach to REFOCUSING. Present it to your students without apology or justification. Pass no judgment on anyone's prior behavior. Simply let the students know that a slightly different kind of consequence will be in place from now on, and proceed to the teach-to about it. Do not be drawn into any philosophical discussions of the merits of the program. (Do not use the term "zero tolerance," which could describe a program in which students are sent to time-out without any warning at all.) Be sure to allow adequate class time for actual walk-throughs of all the expected steps in REFOCUSING, which are both unusual and somewhat complex. Be sure to model or role-play plenty of examples of right, wrong, and "almost" ways to do things. (Don't have time to write behavioral routines? Rick Dahlgren has published "High Expectations and Winning Classroom Behavior: 150 Essential Lesson Plans For Classroom Success" which is a best selling collection of actual lesson plans used by teachers throughout the United States. (See the back of this handbook for more information.)

Now, return to the business of teaching school – but monitor those expected behaviors! If you have been tolerating low-level misbehaviors in the past, you will need to develop a new mindset. As always, you will be appreciative of excellent behaviors – but you will need to become keenly aware of choices that are interfering with learning. Understand that your monitoring of expected behaviors will be in no way mean-spirited. You will simply be ensuring that learning is taking place.

Eventually you will notice a student's misbehavior. After all, if kids already behaved perfectly, we could educate them with video tapes – and we would be out of jobs! So, during either direct instruction, guided practice, or independent practice, you are very likely to spot someone misbehaving, if not today, then one day soon. You may see a student off task, perhaps playing with a forbidden toy. Or you see a student bothering her neighbor, maybe helping herself to a classmate's property. Or you may hear an inappropriate remark, possibly intended as a personal insult to you. Any one of these behaviors would be in violation of your expectations, and any one of them would threaten the integrity of your classroom. The child with the toy cannot learn today's math lesson; the robbed classmate cannot concentrate while her property is being appropriated; and you cannot teach in an atmosphere of challenge and hostility. It is time to act.

This next step is absolutely essential to the success of REFOCUSING. Give a start-up request! "Kevin, I need you to give me your game and begin writing your spelling words." "Marcy, please return Kim's pencils." "Garth, I need you to use respectful language to everyone here, including myself." If you occasionally forget and use a shutdown phrase ("Kevin, stop playing with that game.") it's not the end of the world. At least you have noticed the behavior and prompted the student to change it. You can always count on another chance to phrase a request more positively!

In most cases, the prompt will be enough. Learning and teaching will resume. If at all possible, find an unobtrusive way to immediately reinforce compliance with your request. Anything from a smile to a quiet "thanks" to a "thumbs up" will let the student know that you have noticed and appreciated her good choice. Chances for future good choice making are greatly enhanced!

The student will not always respond to the prompt. (Big surprise, huh?) That game is too intriguing, or those pencils too tempting, or that desire to challenge too strong. This is the moment when, in your calmest voice, you send the student away to REFOCUS. The destination area may be inside your classroom (soloREFOCUS) or in another classroom (buddyREFOCUS), but the student won't have to be told where to go because that has already been explained and actually physically visited during the teach-to about REFOCUSING. Some teachers don't even speak; they have established a hand-signal (thumb toward the door, for example). Judy (who can't always remember which room is the destination for which period) says, "Garth, go to other room, please." Whatever the message, it should be brief, clear, and matter-of-fact. In this fashion, your teaching energy has not been dissolved by a fruitless journey up the "interaction stairway" to the "unbearable limit." As the student departs, learning and teaching resume immediately.

Let us pause right now to partially address the question most frequently asked by teachers who are hearing about this program for the first time. Chances are that it is on your lips, too. "What if the student refuses to go?" Please believe us when we say that, really and truly, it almost never happens. If you think about it for a minute, you can see why. Everybody in the classroom knows exactly what the rules are because you have taught-to those rules. Everybody heard the teacher politely ask the student to follow the rule because a prompt was given. Everybody can see that the student needs to leave so learning can continue. In almost every case we have ever seen, the student has gone to the REFOCUS area without protest or complaint. Which is not to say that there are not refusals sometimes. There are because there are extremely troubled children sometimes. Such a refusal would be a serious matter requiring a very strong and well-thought out plan of action. That plan is explained in Chapter 11.

Whether you or a colleague will be REFOCUSING the student, the student needs to wait respectfully until a teacher finds time to speak with him or her. It is not the teacher's problem that the student has made a poor choice, and the teacher should feel no pressure to interrupt teaching or learning in order to REFOCUS the student. Teaching is the first priority. On the other hand, this process is about learning, not about punishment, so the teacher should not deliberately delay approaching the student, either. Within as brief a time as possible, the teacher motions the waiting student to be seated in the REFOCUS spot (buddyREFOCUS) where he or she completes the REFOCUS form. Recall that the REFOCUS spot is often a desk near the back of the room, away from the students.

REFOCUS questions and their formats vary with age level and teacher preference, but they must always require the student to do three things: identify the inappropriate behavior, recognize the problem it caused, and generate a plan for remediation. The form should always ask for the time of departure and the time returned (buddyREFOCUS). Sample REFOCUS forms can be found in the back of this handbook.

REFOCUS forms may be kept anywhere in the classroom. Rick likes them kept by the door where the REFOCUSING student and teacher can meet, the time of exit written on the form, and the student can immediately commence the REFOCUS process.

At a natural break in instruction the teacher may return to the REFOCUS area and glance at the paper just long enough to ascertain that it has been seriously and properly completed. Or, the teacher may judge from a distance that the student appears to have finished completing the form and motion for the student to meet him or her by the door. If the paper is acceptable, the colleague writes the time in the "time returned" blank and sends the student, paper in hand, back to the sending teacher (or the solo teacher keeps the paper). Back in the home classroom, the student waits quietly for the teacher to evaluate the responses. If the student has correctly identified the misbehavior, recognized the problems it has caused, and formulated a reasonable plan for future behavior, he is welcomed back without fanfare or recrimination. If the answers are inaccurate or unacceptable, the teacher sends the student back to the REFOCUS area to try again.

At no time in this process should any student in either classroom pay any attention to the REFOCUS student, and at no time should the student interact with others. An important part of everyone's learning has been THEIR BUSINESS IS NOT YOUR BUSINESS – in other words, ignore students in the REFOCUS area. But what if someone does interact with the student, even after a teacher request to direct attention to the learning activity? That nosy student must in turn be sent to REFOCUS.

Be prepared to use this exact same process, step-by-step, many times at first. Be prepared even to send several students out within a single hour at first, or one student more than once in a period. Some students just have to find out if you really mean it! Some will need more behavioral instruction than others. We have seen students who have not yet learned how to behave in school needing dozens or even hundreds of REFOCUSES. If you find this happening in your classroom, be patient. Rather than labeling the program a failure, analyze it in terms of student progress. Is the "testing" behavior diminishing? (In our experience, it does.) Is the problem student beginning to make more good choices than before? Is the problem student going to REFOCUS less often than before? Look for progress, not perfection.

Be prepared, as well, to continue to use REFOCUSING throughout the school year – although we think you will be very pleased to see how much less frequently the need arises after a month or so. While it is a very effective discipline program, it will not solve every behavioral problem. What it can do, however, is let you deal so well with low-level misbehaviors that you have time and energy left for major problems, and time and energy for ALL of the children in your classroom. By establishing Time To Teach! in your classroom early on, you will buy a great deal of educational time for the rest of the school year.

Heretofore we have provided a detailed description of the REFOCUS process in writing. Next you will find a diagram (or flow chart) summarizing the steps in sequential order, just as they would happen in our classrooms.

EMERGENT MISBEHAVIOR
(e.g., tapping fingers on desk)

EARLY INTERVENTION

CLASSROOM INTEGRITY QUESTIONS
"Am I able to teach?"
"Are the other students able to learn?"
"Is the student able to learn?"

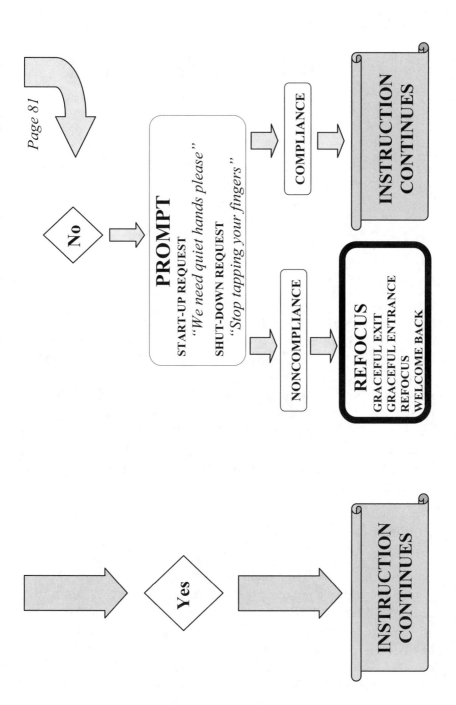

Page 81

No

PROMPT

START-UP REQUEST
"We need quiet hands please"

SHUT-DOWN REQUEST
"Stop tapping your fingers"

COMPLIANCE

INSTRUCTION CONTINUES

NONCOMPLIANCE

REFOCUS
GRACEFUL EXIT
GRACEFUL ENTRANCE
REFOCUS
WELCOME BACK

Yes

INSTRUCTION CONTINUES

CHAPTER 10

ENJOYING TIME TO TEACH

Time To Teach! is a program already in place in thousands of classrooms, schools, and entire school districts around this and other countries. Enthusiasm for the program has spread across the nation. Teachers and administrators use it because it simultaneously improves both discipline and academic performance. They use it because it simultaneously improves both staff morale and school climate. They use it because it simultaneously reduces both teacher stress and student failure. Let's look at benefits of the program for students, teachers, parents, and administrators.

Benefits for Students

Students in Time To Teach! classrooms and schools enjoy a number of advantages over those in either punitive or permissive settings. Above all, they receive respect from their teachers. We all deserve to feel respected, even when we are learning new behaviors. Teachers who have high expectations for student behavior and who hold students accountable for that behavior are respecting their students. Students appreciate the inherent fairness of the system. They appreciate having no surprises about expectations. They appreciate being given credit when they take personal responsibility for their own behavior. They appreciate having teachers respect every student's right to an undisturbed learning environment. Students who are "caught and punished" in traditional ways learn one lesson: if you get caught, you get punished. In some cases, they never know exactly what the offense was, why it angered the teacher, or why it should not happen again – except to escape punishment. Students in settings where misbehaviors go unchecked until teachers reach the unbearable limit learn another lesson: it's okay to misbehave most of the time. Time To Teach! students learn that teachers say what they mean and mean what they say about expected behaviors. When non-compliant students are REFOCUSED, they identify a specific misbehavior, recognize it as a deterrent to learning, and personally create a plan for change. Thus they learn to take personal responsibility for their past and future behavior. Surely learning to take ownership of one's life choices is of great benefit both to our students and to our society!

Improved classroom behavior is as beneficial to students as it is to teachers. Students who are usually well behaved themselves are no longer captive audiences for annoying teacher/student confrontations. They no longer have to donate their valuable learning time to unruly students. They no longer have to listen to lectures about matters that do not concern them. They no longer have to hear embarrassing teacher/student debates, nor are they placed in the uncomfortable position of having to take sides. They no longer have to take some of the fallout when the teacher and student reach the unbearable limit. In short, they can now concentrate on learning rather than on behavior problems. Meantime, the less-than-perfect students are quite surprised and secretly pleased to find themselves learning (over time, remember!) how to behave. Every student benefits when classroom behavior improves.

With that improved behavior comes heightened self-esteem. Webster's defines self-esteem as "belief in oneself; self-respect." When teachers respect their students, when interactions about behavior are quiet and relatively private rather than loud and public, the stage for increased self-esteem has been set. And when children learn how to meet high expectations for behavior, when they come to believe in their own ability to change their behavioral patterns – that is when they can feel honest pride in their own accomplishments. Time To Teach! helps children achieve true self-esteem.

An amazing phenomenon of this program is that, over time, it usually gets even extremely resistant students "down to work." All teachers have had students who put incredible energy into not working. No amount of pleading, ordering, or punishing seems to budge them. But when such "refusniks" find themselves REFOCUSING repeatedly as long as they remain off-task, they gradually and begrudgingly move into the "on-task mode." (Maybe they decide that if they are going to have to spend so much time writing on forms, they might as well be doing something more interesting.) For whatever reasons, Time To Teach! kids are motivated to get to work.

In traditional models of discipline, students would often be put out in the hall or sent to the office. Hallways and offices are not learning environments. Under Time To Teach, students are always in a learning environment – even those who are REFOCUSING. Although they may be momentarily missing part of a lesson in their home classroom, they are busily learning an essential prerequisite to learning: proper learning behavior. All students are enjoying classrooms in which uninterrupted learning is the order of the day. Students in such an environment can enjoy maximum time to learn.

Benefits for Teachers

Teaching school has always been a stressful occupation. Some say that only air traffic controllers face more demands or greater responsibility. Moreover, few laymen would presume to critique the work of an air traffic controller, but sometimes it seems as if everyone is an expert on how teachers should do their jobs. It is a tribute to professional dedication (or possibly insanity!) that we stick it out. Yet many of us do remain in the classroom, apparently because we are crazy enough to love what we do and to care about our students. Increasingly, however, potential teachers are choosing other occupations and current teachers are leaving the profession. The biggest reason for this exodus from teaching is stress, the source of which is lack of discipline. We hear it over and over again – how can you survive in a situation where there is no discipline? It is our opinion that no teacher should be expected to survive in a setting without discipline. Because Time To Teach! is an effective discipline system, it significantly reduces teacher stress. Teacher energy formerly drained by repeated misbehavior can be poured into instructional duties. Stress reduction is the benefit that most new users of Time To Teach! notice first.

Because Time To Teach! is based on fair and positive interactions with students, it allows teachers to maintain a positive tone, not only in their classrooms, but in their own hearts as well. Tone certainly impacts the rate and quality of learning in a classroom – and it impacts our personal and professional lives as well. Eliminating the negative and accentuating the positive are big benefits of Time To Teach!

One of the biggest contributors to that positive atmosphere is the elimination of repeated warnings escalating to the unbearable limit.

Teachers who once dreaded the last quarter of the year because they knew it held "show-downs" are finding it to be the most productive and least stressful time of the year. They find that by consistently and productively addressing low-level behaviors, they have prevented the emergence of most high-level behaviors. This program prevents teachers from reaching the unbearable limit. What a great place not to go to!

Having students write their own REFOCUS forms, which include name, date, and a specific description of their misbehavior (as well as their analysis and plan), turns out to save teachers an enormous amount of time previously spent on documentation. Other discipline systems require teachers to keep all kinds of lists documenting who was warned how many times about what, or to write elaborate referrals to an administrator before a problem can be addressed, or to carefully document every teacher/student interaction. Under Time To Teach, the student does all of this detailed documenting. All the teacher need do is save the REFOCUS papers, being sure to safeguard their privacy. Those papers are useful in a number of ways. For example, teammates who share a troubled student might pool the child's REFOCUS forms as they problem-solve together. Or a teacher might share a struggling student's forms with a counselor or administrator. The forms are particularly valuable at parent conferences, especially with parents who have a hard time believing that their child would be guilty of the infractions described by a teacher. It is hard to contradict admissions in the child's own words, accompanied by dates and times. REFOCUS forms free teachers from tedious documentation.

Building Collegiality

An invaluable bonus of Time To Teach! when working with a "buddy" is the opportunity for collegial teaming. Nowhere can we learn more than from each other, and sharing REFOCUS responsibilities invites learning to take place. Whether piloting the program or continuing it through many years, teachers continually need to confer, monitor, and adjust. This program encourages collegial cooperation at a very meaningful level, and we are continually informed by scores and scores of schools across the nation that they have *never* implemented any program that promoted building collegiality like the Time To Teach! program. Not only are student/student and student/teacher relationships better in these schools, but teacher/teacher relationships are also thriving in Time To Teach! schools.

Benefits for Parents

Parents who understand how Time To Teach! works are among the program's strongest supporters. Above all, parents appreciate their children being in an orderly, disciplined classroom. After school, they are glad to greet happy and productive kids rather than ones frustrated by a day spent in a chaotic classroom. They are impressed when they see evidence of lots of learning and very few discipline problems.

For the parents of a child with a history of problem behavior, the program is truly a gift. Parents accustomed to frequent negative phone calls from teachers are pleased to receive positive messages for a change. Instead of a request from the teacher for the parent to "do something" about the child's classroom behavior, parents may get a report about their child's progress in identifying and changing inappropriate behaviors. Instead of constantly being contacted by the office, they may find themselves in occasional parent conferences using the child's REFOCUS forms as helpful sources of specific information. Instead of being asked to believe a teacher's account of a particular incident, they can work from the child's written account of the event. They can appreciate that their child is being held accountable for low-level behaviors while being precluded from the "high level" zone. Parents whose kids have been struggling with behavior feel encouraged when their children receive more and more positive attention and get into less and less trouble at school.

Sometimes parents will question the wisdom of their child's being sent frequently to REFOCUS, especially when it is in another classroom (buddyREFOCUS). In helping parents understand the value of the program, attention should be paid to several factors. First is that the child knows the expectations yet is choosing not to meet them, even after a start-up request. Second is that teachers do their best to keep the REFOCUS time short. Third, if the rate of frequency of trips to "the other room" is increasing, then indeed there may be a serious problem needing to be addressed in some other setting. On the other hand, if that rate of frequency has been decreasing, then clearly the child is showing improvement. The goal is growth, not perfection. Parents can appreciate seeing evidence that the child is improving.

Another important argument for the wisdom of this system is that, even though she is missing the lesson in her own room, the child is in a learning environment during REFOCUS, as opposed to being out in the hall or in the office. Thus she has a chance of learning something, as opposed to nothing. She is a passive learner while in REFOCUS, but nonetheless she remains in a learning environment. These points usually make good sense to concerned parents.

Benefits for Administrators

One of our biggest challenges with this program is convincing administrators not to mandate it to their staffs. Change, we believe, should come from within an organization rather from the top down, so we strongly urge administrators to offer Time To

Teach! as an option, allowing teachers who pilot it successfully to sell it to the rest of the staff – or not. But there is a reason that administrators love the program so much that they want to require it. Time To Teach! relieves them of petty disciplinary responsibilities and frees them to supervise education. It allows them to spend positive time with students for a change, getting to know all of them instead of just a few. It brings them greater parent support. It lowers administrative stress levels along with that of teachers. It allows them to actually supervise instruction, review curriculum, and develop new programs. Time To Teach! gives them time to do what they were hired to do!

This is a program of proven benefit to students, teachers, parents, and administrators. Maybe it is time to put it to work in your classroom or school.

CHAPTER 11

TIME TO QUESTION

Here are the most frequently asked questions about Time To Teach, in descending order of frequency. We have tried to answer as honestly and thoroughly as possible.

Q: What if the student refuses to go?

A: This is always the first question asked! For that reason, we have already partially addressed it in Chapter 9, explaining that refusals are extremely rare because students are very clear about the fairness of the process. Nevertheless, we admitted, we have known a few students who have defied a teacher's direction to go to the REFOCUS area, and we know that you, too, could encounter such resistance. Such a refusal would be an extremely serious matter. Your response would depend on what arrangements you have in your building, which in turn depends on the degree of support you have from your principal. Let's look at various scenarios, from best case to worst case.

Best Case Scenario:

Your entire building (or maybe even your entire district) has adopted Time To Teach! as its school-wide discipline plan. <u>All the teachers use it</u>. Students are accustomed to the REFOCUS process in all classes and in all shared areas (hallways, cafeteria, playground) of the school. Your staff has an emergency plan to be implemented if ever a student refuses to go to a REFOCUS area. It goes like this:

1. Staff member ignores the refusing child and signals office (ex. intercom, phone, runner, etc.).

2. Office immediately sends trained staff (any available combination of administrators, counselors, secretaries, custodians, para-professionals) to the classroom. They arrive in a calm fashion, enter the room and all start working with the children in the classroom – paying no special attention to the "disrupter."

3. Teacher, still ignoring the refusing child, begins removing the audience by directing one of "the team" to take her entire class, with whatever materials they can manage, to the nearest available learning space away from the classroom. NOTE: The class never goes to someplace "fun." It is important for the class to continue learning, both to reinforce the principle that learning comes first and to prevent other students from choosing refusal behavior in order to give the class a break from learning.

4. Meantime, the "team members" have calmly and non-challengingly placed themselves near the refusing student, patiently awaiting the departure of adult and class. They engage with the child as little as possible, either verbally or physically.

5. Once the audience of classmates has departed, the adults use whatever legal means necessary to escort the child to the office.

Chances are good that the child will be willing to walk with them cooperatively, but if necessary staff will take the child or if necessary even call law enforcement to assist. Be willing to wait a few minutes. Faced with such a calm and positive response, and with so many adults in the classroom, nearly all students will make the right choice.

6. The principal sets consequences according to previously established policy regarding serious infractions. We would expect the matter to be taken extremely seriously and the consequences to be severe. We would also hope that the REFOCUS process would continue at this level, because the opportunity for learning should never stop (a part of our full-day training centers around the emergency response, and how to execute it with maximum success and minimal anxiety. You can also order: "Emergency Intervention – Five Immediate Actions Steps To Take When Confronted By The Verbally or Physically Aggressive Student!").

Middle of the Road Scenario:

You and one or more colleagues are piloting this program. You have your principal's support and have thoroughly briefed her about the program. She is aware that a student's refusal to go to REFOCUS would be an extremely serious disciplinary matter. You know from past experience that you can count on her to back you. Together, you have designed an immediate and appropriately serious plan of action including an element of learning as well as a consequence of suitable magnitude. Possible plans include the one outlined above, a traditional referral to the office, or something in between. For example, a lone administrator could escort the student to the office. Other plans might be worked out in keeping with school policy and administrative choice. The important thing to recognize is that in refusing to go to the REFOCUS area, the child has elected to trade the learning environment for the office.

Worst-Case Scenario:

Being one of the bravest yet most innovative teachers in the world, you are trying this program solo. Your administrators are skeptical and either unable or unwilling to back you up. Nevertheless, things have been going very well for months. However, after ignoring your positive start-up request, an agitated student with a history of inappropriate behavior has refused to go to the REFOCUS area. You must do whatever has the best chance of preventing a violent confrontation. You may send the student to the office or ask the office to come for the student. If violence looms, you may need to take your entire class out of the room and then send for an administrator. In any case, do as much as possible to see that the student's refusal is treated as a serious infraction.

Q: What if the student goes somewhere else instead of to the REFOCUS area?

A: We do everything possible to prevent this. We teach the procedures very thoroughly before we ever send any child to REFOCUS. We explain the route and walk it together. We try to locate the area as close as possible to the home classroom, though of course this is not always possible. (Some teachers successfully send students clear across the school for REFOCUSING.) We insist that departure and return times be written on the forms. Teachers send the student actually carrying the form, having already written the departure time on it in ink. (Here, it would be important to stress that the student may not write on the paper without the receiving teacher's permission.) We can give the REFOCUS form an agreed-upon appearance (color of paper, certain clipboard, etc.) telling everyone where the student should be headed, as well as preventing folks from unwittingly engaging with that child.

Fact of the matter is, though, in almost all cases students do go directly to the area upon request. They are motivated to do so by group dynamics; in other words, they know that their classmates as well as their teacher are expecting them to go. Another motivator is the inherent fairness of the request – which is not to say that they like it, only that they see it as fair. Savvy teachers will observe known wanderers more carefully as they head out. For whatever reasons (childish belief in teachers' X ray eyes?), wandering seldom happens.

If, however, a child deliberately goes to a destination other than the REFOCUS area, the matter should be treated very seriously. Teachers should exercise professional judgment about suitable consequences. Sometimes the appropriate consequence would be further REFOCUS, but in some cases the student's choice to go elsewhere (e.g., outside the building) might constitute as grave infraction as a refusal to go and would be handled accordingly.

Q: What if the same student is REFOCUSED time after time?

A: This is not really a "what if." This is a given. You will have some of these. They are the students who once took you to the unbearable limit. Now, they REFOCUS a great deal. Clearly, they have a great deal to learn about how to behave in a learning environment. We can view this learning as a far better use of everyone's time than constant disruption or trips to the office.

Nonetheless, it is also a good idea to put some procedures in place to use along with REFOCUSING when a child is a "frequent offender." Some teachers establish a formula and begin developing additional consequences after a certain number of REFOCUSES per day, or week, or quarter, or whatever. Others are less structured about it but invoke additional consequences when professional judgment says it's time. Here are some possibilities:

The first consequence, a parent contact, is not really an option. Parents deserve to know about it if their child is taking advantage of this unique learning opportunity on a regular basis. They need to understand that, although the child has not been being punished, she has been missing time from class in order to learn appropriate behaviors. They also deserve to know exactly what behaviors the child is working on. And if the child has missed important work or instruction, make-up time may be needed either at home or at school. Of course, the child's REFOCUS forms help teachers and parents seek solutions to behavior problems during conferences.

Additionally, teachers sometimes impose traditional consequences such as detention, especially if they are concerned about the student's academic progress. It is perfectly acceptable to use such consequences as long as REFOCUSING is also used whenever needed.

As noted earlier, however, it is essential to analyze the frequency of a student's REFOCUSING. It is very easy for one teacher or several to take a look at the forms. Is the student repeating the same misbehavior again and again, more and more often? Or are the misbehaviors less and less frequent? If the incidents are increasingly frequent, a serious behavioral learning problem exists, requiring immediate attention from as many skilled professionals as your school can muster. Mere classroom teachers are doing the best they can with this young person, but they need to insist on getting further help. If help is not forthcoming, they can at least be grateful for a discipline program that may well save both teacher and student from a dangerous and upsetting blow-up.

With behavior as well with academics, students learn at varying rates. Be patient with gradual progress in "slow learners." We have seen some young people with highly challenging behavior patterns absolutely transformed over the course of a year or two in this program. Expect progress, not instant perfection.

Q: What if the student misbehaves in REFOCUS?

A: This is a very rare occurrence. Typical REFOCUS behavior is to try to be as inconspicuous as possible. However, not all kids are typical, and some do misbehave. If the misbehavior is extremely rebellious and/or disruptive, take it as a refusal to go to REFOCUS and implement the emergency plan. If it is less serious, give the student a start-up request (Example: "I expect you to be sitting silently.") If he remains non-compliant, use your professional judgment to decide whether to go to emergency mode or just to notify the sending teacher. (Usually, teachers confer later about these almost-but-not-quite situations and consequent the misbehaviors as needed.)

Q: What if other students interact with the visitor?

A: Those students have just volunteered to go to REFOCUS. Be sure to honor that request! (Remember how everyone role-modeled THEIR BUSINESS IS NOT YOUR BUSINESS during the original teach-to? Students know the expectation.)

Q: What if more than one student needs REFOCUSING at the same time?

A: This is possible. It can happen in one of two ways. One is that the classroom teacher has a second or even third student ignore a start-up request while number one is still out. (This is likeliest to happen early in the implementation of the program.) The teacher should feel perfectly comfortable to send those students to REFOCUS. However, they do not go to the same place. The first student goes to your REFOCUS buddy, another would stay and use the REFOCUS table in your room and another would find a "spot" within your room to REFOCUS. Never send all three to the buddy teacher to REFOCUS at the same time. You wouldn't have a buddy teacher for long!

The other way is that the buddy teacher receives more than one student at a time. The students could come from two or three different teachers at once. (This will not occur at the elementary level as we all have only one buddy teacher. At the secondary level, we may use different buddy teachers depending upon the time of day.) This happened to Judy once (on a Friday afternoon, naturally). One was at the REFOCUS table in the back of the room. Number two went to the teacher's desk. Number three sat in an empty student desk. She is proud to report that her students conscientiously ignored all three of them. Eventually, she sent them back one at a time. Such traffic jams are possible but very uncommon.

Q: What if I appear weak because I send so many students to REFOCUS?

A: Teachers regularly struggle with this self-esteem issue. Many of us were taught in our teacher-training classes that our brilliant teaching strategies and fascinating curriculum would prevent discipline problems before they could ever begin. No wonder that having a student exhibit less than perfect behavior during one of our award-winning lessons feels like condemning evidence of incompetence! We are not sure what century or planet those teacher-trainers are from, but it wasn't Planet Earth at the turn of the second millennium. All teachers encounter difficult students! No teacher can be all things to all kids all the time! Not all students know everything they should about proper learning behavior! Some of the finest teachers we know are the biggest proponents of this program because it has increased their already high job satisfaction to a pinnacle they had never dreamed possible.

www.timetoteach.com & www.goteachergo.com

Teachers working together must discuss this issue of mutually supporting one another. All involved must philosophically accept the appropriateness of these interventions. All must be willing to trust a colleague's professional judgment in sending a student to REFOCUS. All must be willing to receive and process students in a non-punitive way. Above all, no one must ever undermine a colleague by passing judgment on a teacher's decision-making in the presence of students! Certainly, a receiving teacher should never audibly question the wisdom of the sending teacher – although it might be a professional responsibility to discuss matters of real concern with the colleague at a later date.

Realistically, of course, it would certainly be possible for a teacher to overuse the program. If you find this happening to you, review the basics. Do you orchestrate non-contingent as well as contingent interactions with students? Have you thoroughly "taught to" expectations? Are you using start-up prompts? Are you being fair and consistent in monitoring behavior and intervening when called for? And is your curriculum interesting and challenging, yet not too frustrating?

Some honest self-assessment may pinpoint a target for improvement.

Q: What are some ways to misuse this program?

A: The most common misuse of Time To Teach! is making it punitive. REFOCUSING is a learning process, not a punishing process. Students are REFOCUSED when something is "beginning to interfere" with their learning. If a receiving teacher deliberately waits a very long time before REFOCUSING a student (as opposed to truly being too busy), that teacher is acting punitively. If teachers are angry, accusatory, judgmental, sarcastic, etc., they are acting punitively. This program changes behavior most effectively when it is clearly used as a teaching strategy, not as a punishment.

Another misuse is inconsistency. Teachers need to do their level best to monitor behavior consistently, although we never want to get hooked into debating "He was doing it, too!" Such accusations may indicate a real need to watch the whole class, not just the known "trouble-makers."

Another common error is failure to give one positive start-up request. Regular omission of that request creates a punitive system and fosters student resentment.

The opposite side of that coin is giving more than one start-up request. More than one equals a repeated warning, or multiple request, which is what this program is designed to eliminate.

The good news is that even a misused version of Time To Teach! can be an improvement over former systems (or non-systems). Example: A sixth-grade teacher was engaged in constant verbal wrangles with "smart-mouthed girls." As their debates escalated, he would grow increasingly negative and sarcastic while they would grow more defensive and inappropriate. The entire class was suffering from this negative atmosphere, as was the teacher's blood pressure. Then he joined his colleagues in using REFOCUSING. Philosophically, he never fully embraced the program. He didn't teach to expectations thoroughly, nor did he give positive start-up requests. What he did do was send the girls to REFOCUS as soon as he heard a "smart remark." Even though he was omitting essential elements of the program, and even though the girls could have made far more progress with a more learning-based approach, things were far better in the classroom. Why? Because the negative interactions between teacher and students had stopped. All of the students were calmer, the teacher's blood pressure dropped, and more learning was happening. We do not recommend misusing Time To Teach, but neither do we expect instant perfection from teachers any more than from students. Implementing this program, like learning appropriate behavior, is a process over time.

CHAPTER 12

TIME TO EXPAND

TEACHERS:
SAVE THIS CHAPTER UNTIL YOU ARE READY FOR IT

ADMINISTRATORS:
READ THIS NOW

This chapter is intended for those zealots who have successfully piloted Time To Teach! in their own classrooms and are feeling called to evangelize. It is also for those administrators who see how well the program is working in some classrooms and would love to see it adopted throughout the school. If you are one of those zealous teachers or administrators, dive in. If not, put this chapter on hold for now – but if the spirit calls you later, remember to read it!

Time To Teach, like most good things in life, is best advertised first by example and then by word of mouth. That is one reason that the impetus for this program should come from the classroom rather than from the office. Teachers, notoriously jaded about fads and buzzwords in education, are very leery of programs mandated from above. They are much more likely to trust one another, especially about a core issue like discipline. Many of them need to see this program working for colleagues before they feel comfortable trying it themselves. That's why we respectfully recommend that school boards and administrators not mandate the program. Here, however, are our recommendations for ways in which teachers or administrators could appropriately "spread the gospel" about Time To Teach.

Earlier we explained how a teacher can enlist the aid of a "buddy" either as a full-fledged co-pilot of REFOCUS or as a receiving teacher only. Together, these two must become sold on the program as they implement it. This takes at least a semester and probably a full school year. If solid groundwork of positive interactions, clear expectations and thorough teach-to's is laid, and if those expectations are consistently and fairly enforced through REFOCUSING, the program will succeed, and these two teachers will be eager to spread the word.

As there are many paths to enlightenment, so there are many paths to a school-wide discipline program. In some schools, the original "pilots" of Time To Teach! will enlist other teachers – perhaps through their grade level, pod, or department – to adopt the program during the next school year or after the holiday break. In other situations, the groundbreakers may feel comfortable asking their principals for permission to present the program, as an option, to the whole staff. We cannot stress enough how important it is to give teachers a choice in this matter! Accept from the beginning that some teachers on staff may never embrace this program. If they already have effective, respectful discipline plans in place, no problem. If chaos reigns in their classrooms, an administrative problem exists and needs to be addressed by administrators – who might then appropriately encourage the teacher to try this plan.

Good products sell themselves, and Time To Teach! does just that. Chances are that when teachers hear about the benefits of the program from someone they trust, they will want to give it a try themselves. Once there is a site-based decision to adopt the program, someone needs to be sure that adequate time is spent on the following:

1. In-Servicing Staff

A school-wide discipline program must truly be implemented school-wide. Even though some teachers may choose not to send their classroom students to REFOCUS, every staff member should agree to use the REFOCUSING process in shared areas of the school. Therefore, adequate time should be spent in training the entire staff, from custodians to principal, to use Time To Teach. Consult page 110 of this handbook for more information on how and why to bring a master teacher/trainer and The Center For Teacher Effectiveness' nationally acclaimed Time To Teach! program to your school! **We urge you to order a free promotional video on the Time To Teach! program today.** Call 800 438-1808 to order the free promotional video ($5.00 shipping).

2. Identifying Building Absolutes

Absolutes are identified behaviors requiring immediate administrative intervention and are never dealt with by teachers or paraprofessionals. Absolutes are those egregious behaviors that simply will not ever be tolerated in your district, building, or classroom, with no exceptions. Absolutes should be few in number but powerful in message. In common terms, behavior absolutes describe the point at which you "draw a line in the sand"

and will not retreat. Typically, absolutes forbid weapons, drugs and alcohol, and violence – both verbal and physical. These absolutes should be determined by an entire staff, including the students (you might be amazed how similar their views are to yours when it comes to what is and is not acceptable) and be based on a combination of district policy and building preference.

Of course, in blending district policy with building preference, district policy cannot be abridged. If district policy forbids weapons, building policy must do the same. Perhaps, though, a school wants to curb violence of any kind. In writing their absolutes, they might expand a district policy asserting "zero tolerance for weapons" to read "zero tolerance for anything that looks or sounds like violence." A building should review its special circumstances and formulate a set of absolutes focused on extremely serious behaviors.

Students who violate absolutes will not be REFOCUSED. Their cases will go straight to administration or law enforcement, and parents will be notified. Consequences will range from suspension to referral to law enforcement. With that in mind, be sure that the battle triggered by your absolutes is worth fighting. Edicts against wearing hats in the building or chewing gum in class might be logical and worthwhile building rules, but not building absolutes. Be willing as a staff to save the absolutes for truly egregious infractions.

3. Teaching to Absolutes

Once determined by the staff, building absolutes must be taught to and enforced as a building team. There are no options here. Every teacher in the building should teach to the absolutes on the same day or days, beginning if possible on the first day of school. A system should be in place to assure that absentees hear the lesson upon their return. Parents should be informed of the absolutes in writing. Any staff member witnessing a violation of an absolute must send the perpetrator directly to an administrator, and the administrator must deal with that perpetrator aggressively. Serious infractions must be treated seriously.

4. Designing a School-Wide Management Plan

Conducting an Ecological Analysis

Just as a teacher analyzes the physical arrangement of a classroom, a staff needs to conduct an "ecological analysis" of its building, grounds, and transportation system. The guiding questions should be:

> *Where are our students experiencing the most difficulty?*
> *Why are they experiencing difficulty there?*
> *What changes can help them?*

Problem areas often include campus borders, playgrounds, lunchroom, entrances and exits, drinking fountains, restrooms, and hallways. Problem systems usually include sequence of eating and playing, proximity of various age groups, hallway traffic patterns, wait times, and bells. If safety around drinking fountains is a problem, paint lines around the fountains and allow "one-at-a-time" only within that space. If children are leaving their lunches uneaten because they are in a hurry to get outside and play, send them out to play before they eat! Schools using this reversal of the traditional sequence find that, when lunch follows a play period, children eat better, behave better in the cafeteria, and settle down faster upon return to class.

5. Teaching to Shared Areas and Routines

In an orderly school, just as in an orderly classroom, children need to know the expectations, and we cannot assume that they already do. We must systematically teach to our school-wide expectations. Therefore, the staff must identify shared areas, common routines, and typical activities outside the classroom. For each one, someone must design a school-wide lesson to be taught as early as possible in the school year. At one middle school, for instance, every teacher presents the identical lesson on cafeteria behavior, including traffic patterns and line-up behavior, before lunch on the first day of school. In the same systematic way, they teach to assembly behavior several days before the first assembly of the year. Student cafeteria and assembly behavior has improved immensely. School-wide teach-to's covering shared routines can dramatically reduce the incidence of problem behavior in your school!

6. REFOCUSING Throughout the Building

Many teachers are satisfied with behavior within their own classrooms but frustrated by the behavior of students (their own or not) in hallways, on the playground, etc. Adopting Time To Teach! school-wide enables every staff member to deal more effectively with inappropriate low-level behaviors with any student in any setting. For example, all students in the school have been taught to make trips to the restroom without disturbing classes in session. A student from another class bounces past your open classroom door, swinging a bathroom pass and singing loudly, distracting your students from their learning. In the past, you might have hesitated to do anything, or at best would have scolded the student. Today, you ask the student to be seated at the REFOCUS area in your classroom and take her through the process. Once she identifies her behavior and a plan for the future, send her back to class, making sure that she does get to use the bathroom.

Other scenarios might occur in crowded hallways or on the playground. Here, where forms may not be handy, students can be asked to stand against a wall and then REFOCUSED verbally. Teachers wanting written documentation can write the incident up at their earliest opportunity in their own words – on a REFOCUS form.

Some schools develop maps or schedules of REFOCUS destination areas. For example, adult playground or cafeteria monitors might send students to a nearby, staffed location for REFOCUSING. However, since REFOCUS is about learning, such a destination should not be a space usually devoted to punishment. Every school is unique and will develop its own unique plan; the important thing is to develop it, teach to it, and use it consistently.

7. Organize Buddies

Scheduling classes is a complicated matter, and it is rare to find two nearby teachers with identical schedules. Therefore it is usually practical to work out a map or schedule of sending and receiving teachers on a period by period basis. Furthermore, some schools send students to different grades for REFOCUS, while in others, teachers prefer to organize REFOCUSING within interdisciplinary teams in the same grade. These are individual decisions based on unique characteristics of your school. Whatever your arrangements, you will keep what works and change the rest.

Once the basics are in place, put this program to work. We think that you will soon be enjoying an entire school in which students have time to learn and administrators have time to administer because teachers have Time To Teach!

For more information on how to implement building-wide, you might want to order Time To Teach! – on DVD. More information on this 5-plus hour DVD is located at the end of this handbook.

Read on to discover just how powerful Time To Teach! is when implemented building-wide. . . .

The Bryan School Story

Ten years ago The Center For Teacher Effectiveness and Rick Dahlgren began training at Bryan School. The following spring marked the beginning of one of the most exciting success stories in public education.

Bryan had a history of low test scores and a reputation of behavior problems, lack of parent involvement, vandalism and a "second class" mentality. Over the summer, a fellow by the name of John House was named principal. (He is now a national trainer and motivational speaker for The Center For Teacher Effectiveness). John met with the students, staff, and parents and found all three groups wanting to reduce problem behavior and improve academic standards. Rick Dahlgren trained the staff – not just the teaching staff, but the entire staff. The school organized summer meetings and analyzed problem areas, wrote student expectations (teach-to's) and established building absolutes.

Change came fast. The students were greeted with substantial noncontingent interaction, or unconditional positive regard, by a staff with a renewed vision – which included caring enough about the students to discipline them and to set expectations that were clear, concise and enforceable.

Office referrals and suspensions dropped dramatically during the second semester. There had been more than 100 office referrals in May of the previous year. Following Time To Teach! implementation, there were fewer than 30 referrals in September **and** October and only 7 in January **and** February! Suspensions dropped from 14 in September to an average of **one per month** for the remainder of the year! Parent and community members began volunteering more than ever before. Test scores skyrocketed:

ITBS Testing Results
Percentiles Before and After Time To Teach!

Before   After *(following year, same students)*

Grade 3

	Before		After		
Reading	36	Reading	58	*plus 22*
	22		**59**	***plus 37***
Language	38	Language	50	*plus 12*
	23		**43**	***plus 20***
Math	35	Math	69	*plus 34!*
	24		**75**	***plus 51***

(Note: the top percentile in each of the three sections represents Bryan's percentile ranking among schools within its own school district, while the bottom percentile in each of the three sections **(bold)** represents Bryan's percentile ranking among schools nationally.)

John House and his staff have opened the doors of Bryan School to visiting educators from across the United States. On a weekly basis they welcome visitors from Idaho, Montana, Wyoming, Utah, Oregon, Washington, Colorado, Oklahoma, etc. . . .They come. . .because they have heard of the story of Bryan School.

www.timetoteach.com & *www.goteachergo.com*

When John House says Time To Teach! works, he speaks from first-hand experience. Would you like to talk with him? Contact The Center For Teacher Effectiveness for details.

John House is now retired, but the program remains strong today in Bryan...**ten years later!** We have many more success stories to share.

Bring Time To Teach! To Your School

Rick Dahlgren is at the core of a group of several dozen people training for The Center For Teacher Effectiveness. The Center has carefully selected top-notch master teachers to join our elite team of national trainers. They come from elementary, middle and high school levels. They bring a unique blend of experience (only active teachers are invited to train), theory and entertainment to The Center For Teacher Effectiveness. With experience in every sector of public education from kindergarten to university classrooms, they draw on "real life" personal experience and *they know what works!* Should you go through a training you will begin the day with courteous giggles, move through open chuckles and into side-splitting belly laughs as these national champions of extemporaneous speaking share anecdotes, data, and practical ideas about classroom and school-wide discipline. For example, hear John or Rick tell the story of taking a school that was the educational equivalent of "Fort Apache - the Bronx" and of turning it into an institution honored by the state as an "Exemplary School."

The Center For Teacher Effectiveness presents nationally and internationally to packed audiences. Discipline can be **fun**...and these top notch trainers will tell you **why**...and show you **how!** Call 800 438-1808 for more information.

REFOCUS© Form

(you may change and reproduce this form)

(Middle/Secondary Level)

Student Name _____ Date _____

Time left homeroom: _____ Time left buddy: _____

Period: _____

Teacher who sent you _____

1. What was your behavior?

I was _____

_____

_____

2. What did you want?

I wanted _____

3. What problem(s) did your behavior cause for you, your classmates, and/or your teacher?

My behavior _____

_____

_____

4. How do you plan to change your behavior in the future?

I will _____

_____

_____

5. I am ready to return to class: "Check" One → YES ☐   NO ☐

www.timetoteach.com & www.goteachergo.com

REFOCUS© Form

(you may change and reproduce this form)

(Intermediate/Primary)

Date _____

Student Name _____

Time left homeroom: _____

Time left buddy: _____

1. What was your behavior?

I Was _____

_____

_____

2. **What did you want?**

I wanted_____

_____

_____

3. **What will you do next time?**

I will_____

_____

_____

4. **I am ready to return to class:** "Check" One → **YES** ☐ **NO** ☐

www.timetoteach.com & www.goteachergo.com

REFOCUS© Form

(you may change and reproduce this form)

(Kindergarten/First Grade)

(Often done verbally. The teacher may choose to document the student's answers in writing)

What did you do?

What did you want?

What will you do when you join your class?

Can you do it?

Name: _____

Date: _____

Time To Teach!
Essential Components

❑ 1. A Strong Belief System - CHAPTER I

❑ 2. Effective Child Management Strategies - CHAPTER II

❑ 3. Self-Control - CHAPTER III

❑ 4. Proper Classroom Arrangement - CHAPTER IV

❑ 5. Unconditional Positive Regard - CHAPTER V

❑ 6. Teach To Expectations - CHAPTER VI

❑ 7. Other Reactive (Prevention) Strategies - CHAPTER VII

❑ 8. REFOCUS - CHAPTER VIII & IX
    a. Early Intervention
    b. Classroom Integrity Questions
    c. Prompting
    d. Refocusing
       1. Graceful Exit
       2. Graceful Entrance
       3. REFOCUS Moment
       4. Welcome Back
          a. REFOCUSING non-judgmentally

Time For A Present

THE PRESENT

Imagine there is a bank that credits your account each morning with $86,400. It carries over no balance from day to day. Every evening it deletes whatever part of the balance you failed to use during the day. What would you do? Draw out every cent, of course! Each of us has such a bank.

Its name is TIME.

Every morning, it credits you with 86,400 seconds. Every night it writes off, as lost, whatever of this you have failed to invest to good purpose. It carries over no balance. It allows no overdraft. Each day it opens a new account for you.

Each night it burns the day's deposits; the loss is yours. There is no going back. There is no drawing against the "tomorrow." You must live in the present on today's deposits. Invest it so as to get from it the utmost in health, happiness, and success! The clock is running. Make the most of today.

To realize the value of ONE YEAR,
ask a student who failed a grade.

To realize the value of ONE MONTH,
ask a mother who gave birth to a pre-mature baby.

To realize the value of ONE WEEK,
ask the editor of a weekly newspaper.

To realize the value of ONE DAY,
ask a daily wage laborer with kids to feed.

www.timetoteach.com & *www.goteachergo.com*

To realize the value of ONE HOUR,
ask the lovers who are waiting to meet.

To realize the value of ONE MINUTE,
ask the man who missed his train.

To realize the value of ONE SECOND,
ask the person who just avoided an accident.

To realize the value of ONE MILLISECOND,
ask the person who won a silver medal in the Olympics.

Treasure every moment that you have! And treasure it more
because you've shared it with someone special—special enough to
share your time. And remember that time waits for no one.
Yesterday is history. Tomorrow is a mystery. Today is a gift.

Author Unknown

Testimonials

"This innovative program is truly a gift to children and teachers. It transformed our school from one on "school improvement status," to a school recognized as a "Distinguished Title I School" by the U.S. Department of Education in 2001. In 26 years of being a principal, I have never seen a program be **accepted and embraced, by all staff members, so quickly.**

I have also seen it work in many other schools across America. I have visited with extensive numbers of principals and teachers who value its effectiveness in making school a more memorable and meaningful experience for all students."

Darrell Rud, President
National Association of Elementary School Principals
2001-2002

"Five blue stars! We have learned how to be firm, yet fair, with our students. I feel confident that I can handle literally any event in my classroom...in a positive fashion."

Deb Ptasky, Grade 9 Teacher

"What a wonderful, kind, yet powerful set of strategies. This is the most powerful solution to problem behavior I've ever heard of! I wish I would have learned this in college."

Nick Mattioda, Grade 2 Teacher

"My principal requested that I attend the Time To Teach seminar...quite frankly, because I was on professional assistance. After struggling for two years with discipline issues, I finally have a plan that will work for myself and my students. I sincerely thank you from the bottom of my heart."

Anonymous, New Teacher

Wow! "Learn how to draw a line in the sand." In your classroom, have high standards and happy students. What more could you ask for?!

ABCnews.com

www.timetoteach.com & *www.goteachergo.com*

"We liked this program so much, we had Rick Dahlgren train in all of our schools!"
Rick Dutton
Director of Education, Denver Public Schools.

"We have a very diverse rural community on an Indian Reservation. 60% of our students are Native American. Some discipline programs tried in past years were not effective, and were not accepted by the parents. With "Time To Teach," we are experiencing tremendous community support, and our teachers have noticed an increase in quality teaching time in their classrooms.

We have witnessed that specifically "teaching-to" expectations, modeling them, and practicing them with students has had a tremendous positive impact, not only on student behavior, but also on student learning.

We now have a positive school climate, overwhelming parent support, and staff appreciation (because they have much more quality time for instruction). Time To Teach makes everything in our school better!"
Jim Gillhouse, Principal

"I am a thirty-year veteran. I thought I'd seen all...done all. Time To Teach has taught me more about successfully managing my classroom than I have learned in my previous thirty years of experience. Maybe I'll sign on for another five years!"
Jim Nolstad, Grade 6 Teacher

"What a great lesson in humanity! This is the third time I've been to a Time To Teach seminar and I learn so much more every time! As promised, they give you Tools for Tomorrow, not just Theory for Thought."
Kari Vickers, School Psychologist

"The Time To Teach program takes a very complex issue (classroom discipline) and reduces it to an understandable, very easy set of strategies that any classroom teacher can use. I can't wait to start school on Monday and try this out!"
Kori Meredith, (Australia) Middle Grade Teacher

www.timetoteach.com & *www.goteachergo.com*

"We brought Time To Teach to Campbell County School District. This program has proven itself to be very successful for our teachers at both the elementary and secondary level. I have heard nothing but positive comments from our teaching staff regarding this program.

As part of my duties with the district, I have the opportunity to supervise the substitute teachers. We have required all of these individuals to go through this training, which has led to their increased success in the classroom! Parents have had very complimentary comments regarding this program as well!"

George E. Mathes, Jr.
Assistant Superintendent For Instruction

"I was a skeptical when I was first approached by two principals about offering Time To Teach within our school district. It seemed too good to be true.

Never in my wildest dreams did I think we would get the response that we did. Veteran teachers of 20+ years said it was the best program they had encountered in their tenure with our district. Without a doubt, this is the single best program we have ever seen.

As our teachers heard about the program, they attended trainings on a volunteer basis! Sound too good to be true? If I hadn't kept the records myself, I would find it hard to believe. Our top teachers praise the program because it has literally given them more time to teach their content, and a process that treats all students fairly and with dignity. One foreign language teacher was astonished to find at the end of the first semester that she was a full month further in her curriculum than in previous years! She attributes that to the fact that Time To Teach eliminated the "pesky" behaviors that previously consumed so much of her teaching time.

I speak for our entire leadership team in saying that this may be the best program available anywhere, for any school!"

Carrylann Goens, Staff Development Director

"When I first learned the Time To Teach strategies and framework, I was immediately hooked! As I see it, Time To

Teach connects many of the varied management programs into one, easy-to-use, friendly-yet-firm, powerful approach.

During summative evaluations this year, numerous teachers noted, unprompted, how positive their classrooms have become using Time To Teach strategies.

In our school, understanding, respecting, and honoring diversity is very important. Time To Teach elegantly honors the uniqueness of every student, in every room!"

Steve Fenton, Principal

"Greetings from the Flathead Indian Reservation. I have been in the field of education for over 15 years, working as a classroom teacher in grades K-12, and as a curriculum specialist. As a tribal member I have had a particular interest in issues of multiculturalism, equity, literacy, and social justice.

In Indian families and communities, children are regarded with the same respect that is afforded to adults. Most often children are taught by example and discipline is thought of as guidance and direction, rather than punishment. Time To Teach operates on a similar belief. Perhaps the most important reason that I embrace the Time To Teach program, is that it is based on the belief that all children deserve to be treated with dignity."

Julie Cajune, Indian Education Coordinator.

Inspirational Quotes

For Teachers

"A teacher affects eternity; he can never tell where his influence stops."
- *Henry Brooks Adams*

"A teacher is one who makes himself progressively unnecessary."
- *Thomas Carruthers*

"A teacher who is attempting to teach, without inspiring the pupil with a desire to learn, is hammering on a cold iron."
- *Horace Mann (1796-1859)*

"Education...is a painful, continual and difficult work to be done in kindness, by watching, by warning, by praise, but above all -- by example."
- *John Ruskin*

"Education's purpose is to replace an empty mind with an open one."
- *Malcolm Forbes*

"Getting things done is not always what is most important. There is value in allowing others to learn, even if the task is not accomplished as quickly, efficiently or effectively."
- *R.D. Clyde*

"It is important that students bring a certain ragamuffin, barefoot, irreverence to their studies; they are not here to worship what is known, but to question it."
- *J. Bronowski, The Ascent of Man*

www.timetoteach.com & *www.goteachergo.com*

"Spoon feeding in the long run teaches us nothing but the shape of the spoon."
- E. M. Forster

"Teachers should guide without dictating, and participate without dominating."
- C.B. Neblette

"The mind is not a vessel to be filled, but a fire to be ignited."
- Plutarch

"There are no difficult students - just students who don't want to do it your way."
- Jane Revell & Susan Norman

"The teacher who is indeed wise does not bid you to enter the house of his wisdom, but rather leads you to the threshold of your mind."
- Kahlil Gibran

"Who dares to teach must never cease to learn."
- John Cotton Dana

"You can't direct the wind but you can adjust the sails."
- Anonymous

For Students

"A turtle makes progress when it sticks its neck out."
- Anonymous

"Don't learn to do, but learn in doing. Let your falls not be on a prepared ground, but let them be bona fide falls in the rough and tumble of the world."
- Samuel Butler (1835–1902)

"Every artist was at first an amateur."
- *Ralph W. Emerson*

"I hear, and I forget. I see, and I remember. I do, and I understand."
- *Chinese Proverb*

"If you always do what you've always done, you'll always get what you've always got."
- *NLP adage*

"One of the greatest discoveries a man makes, one of his great surprises, is to find he can do what he was afraid he could not do."
- *Henry Ford*

"The important thing in life is not the triumph but the struggle."
- *Pierre de Coubertin*

"Teachers open the door, but you must enter by yourself."
- *Chinese Proverb*

"The only dreams impossible to reach are the ones you never pursue."
- *Michael Deckman*

"Worry is misuse of the imagination."
- *Mary Crowley*

"You haven't failed, until you stop trying."
- *Unknown*

Bibliography of Recommended Readings

Coopersmith, S. (1967). The antecedents of self-esteem, San Francisco, CA W.H. Freeman and Company.

Donnellan, A., LaVigna, G., Negri-Shoultz, N., & Fassbender, L. (1988). Progress without punishment. New York and London: Teachers College Press.

Donnellan, A., & LaVigna, G. (1986). Alternatives to punishment. New York, NY: Irvington Publishers, Inc.

Donnellan, A., Mirenda, P., Mesaros, R., & Fassbender, L. (1984). Analyzing the communicative functions of aberrant behavior in JASH, Vol. 9, No. 3, 201-212.

Falvey, M, Forest, M., Pearpoint, J. & Rosenberg, R. (1994). All my life's a circle. Toronto, ON, Canada: Inclusion Press.

Glasser W. (1984). Take effective control of your life. New York, NY: Harper & Row, Publishers.

Glasser, W. (1985). Control theory, New York, NY: Harper - Collins.

Glasser, W. (1986). Control theory in the classroom. New York, NY: Harper & Row, Publishers.

Goldstein, A., & Glick, B. (1987). Aggression replacement training: a comprehensive intervention for aggressive youth. Champaign, IL: Research Press.

Hall, G.E., Wallace, Jr., R.C., & Dossett, W.A. (1972). A developmental conceptualization of the adoption process within educational institutions. Austin, Texas: Research and

Development Center for Teacher Education, The University of Texas.

Jones, V. & Jones, L. (1990). Comprehensive classroom management: motivating and managing students. Boston, MA: Allyn and Bacon.

Keirsey, D. & Bates, M. (1978). Please understand me. Englewood Cliffs, NJ: Prentice Hall.

Kohn, A. (1990). The brighter side of human nature: altruism and empathy in everyday life. Basic Books.

Kunc, N. (1992). The need to belong. In R. Villa, J. Thousand, W. Stainback & S. Stainback (Eds.), Restructuring for caring & effective education. Baltimore, London, Toronto & Sydney: Paul H. Brookes Publishing Company.

Janney, Black, Ferio. (1989). A problem solving approach to challenging behaviors.

Johnson, D.W. & Johnson, R.T. (1984). Cooperation in the classroom. Edina, MN: Interaction Book Company.

Long, N.J & Newman. (1965) Managing surface behaviors of school children

Long, N.J., Morse, W.C., Newman, R.G. (1980). *Conflict in the classroom.* Belmont, CA: Wadsworth Publishing Company.

Lovett, H. (1985). Cognitive counseling for persons with behavioral challenges. NY, CT, & London: Praeger.

McCarthy, B. (1980, 1987). 4MAT system: teaching to learning styles with right/left mode techniques. Barrington, IL: Excel,

Inc.

McGee, J., Menolascino, F., Hobbs, D. & Menousek, P. (1987). Gentle teaching: A non-aversive approach to helping persons with mental retardation. New York, NY: Human Sciences Press, Inc.

McGinnis, E. & Goldstein, A. (1984). 1. Skillstreaming the elementary school child: A guide for teaching prosocial skills, and; 2. Skillstreaming the adolescent. Champaign, IL: Research Press.

Meyer, L. & Evans, I. (1989). Non-aversive intervention for behavior problems: a manual for home and community. Baltimore, London Toronto, Sydney: Paul H. Brookes.

O'Neill, R., Homer, R., Albin, R., Storey, K. & Sprague, J. (1990). Functional analysis of problem behavior: a practical assessment guide. Sycamore, IL: Sycamore Publishing Company.

Peck, M.S. (1993). A world waiting to be born: civility rediscovered. New York, Toronto, London, Sydney & Auckland: Bantam Books.

Samples, B. (1987). Open mind/ whole mind. Torrence, CA: Jalmar Press.

Sizemore, B.A. (1985). "Pitfalls and promises of effective schools research," Journal of Negro Education, 54 269-288.

Smith, J. (1985). Relaxation dynamics. Champaign, IL: Research Press.

Snow, J. (1993). <u>What's really worth doing and how to do it</u>. Toronto, ON, Canada: Inclusion Press.

Tobin, L. (1991). <u>What do you do with a child like this? inside the lives of troubled children</u> USA: Edwards Brothers, Inc.

Topper, Williams, Leo, Hamilton, Fox. (1994). <u>A positive approach to understanding and addressing challenging behaviors.</u>

Warner, Carolyn. <u>The Litany</u>

Wood, G. (1992). <u>Schools that work.</u> New York, NY: Plume, Penguin Books.

Zeph, L. (1986). "The C.H.O.I.C.E. curriculum model: a positive programming and intervention strategy for students with severe behavior problems," presented at the 1986 Annual Conference of the Association for Persons with Severe Handicaps, San Francisco, CA.

More Time To Teach! Materials
Information & Order Form

BOOKS

High Expectations and Winning Classroom Behavior
150 Essential Lesson Plans For Classroom Success!
by Rick Dahlgren

Bell Work
by Rick Dahlgren and Mary Kotnour

Moving From Ordinary to Extraordinary Relationships With Your Students
Creating A Classroom That All Love To Enter
by Rick Dahlgren

Play Cool At School
by Mary Kotnour and Rick Dahlgren

Time To Teach – Training Manual
"Tools for Tomorrow *not just* Theory For Thought"
by Rick Dahlgren

DVD'S

Time To Teach (5+ hrs)
"Tools for Tomorrow *not just* Theory For Thought"
with Rick Dahlgren and other master teachers

Self-Control: Remaining Cool and Responding Right! (2 hrs)
"How to take the right course of action when being challenged"
with Rick Dahlgren

High Expectations and Winning Classroom Behavior (2 hrs)
150 Essential Lesson Plans For Classroom Success!
by Rick Dahlgren

www.timetoteach.com & *www.goteachergo.com*

Emergency Intervention! (1+ hr)
"Five Immediate Action Steps To Take When Confronted By The
Verbally or Physically Aggressive Student!"
with Rick Dahlgren

Moving From Ordinary to Extraordinary (2 hrs)
Relationships With Your Students:
Creating A Classroom That All Love To Enter
with teachers from around America

Time To Teach – School-Wide DVD (8+ hrs)
"Tools for Tomorrow *not just* Theory For Thought"
with Rick Dahlgren and other master teachers

CD

Just for fun! This musical CD was designed to help Time To Teach participants remember what they learned during our training. The music is fun, and the lyrics are written just for teachers. It is a one of a kind item.

Time To Teach Trainings
School Trainings

- ## One-Day On-Site School Trainings

Fast-paced and **filled with scores and scores of useful and practical strategies**. Especially known to be motivating, refreshing, humorous, and packed with ideas that your teachers can use tomorrow! Taught by "active duty" elite K-12 teachers who know what you face and who know how to help!

- ## Two-Day On-Site School Trainings

1) Learn how to "teach to" classroom- and school-wide expectations and routines, which will improve your student's performance everywhere in the school building.

2) Learn how to arrange and position students for maximum achievement, both inside and outside of the classroom. Arranging students properly in the classroom can make the teacher the focus of attention. Proper arrangement in lines and in "shared areas" is also critical. Learn how, when, where and why to arrange students for maximum performance.

3) Learn positive and effective communication skills. Learn how to assertively communicate with your students, and to detect and avoid conflict. Learn strategies to increase teaching time and finish all tasks important to you.

4) Use proven methods to deal with serious, challenging behavior. Learn how to quickly, quietly, and effectively deal with the "out-of-control" student. Eliminate acting out by identifying "triggers" and intervening early.

5) Learn how to Use "REFOCUS." Learn to easily use the most powerful solution to problem behavior ever developed. Identify and avert problem situations before they happen. Use techniques to confidently meet challenging student behavior with positive results.

www.timetoteach.com & *www.goteachergo.com*

6) Identify environmental conditions that hamper student performance. Learn how noise, crowds, heat, waiting, and other external factors can generate misbehavior, and then learn what you can do to minimize these distractions so you can teach!

7) Build positive relationships. Learn how to "teach with passion and manage with compassion."

8) Learn how to respond calmly and consistently. Learn strategies to identify and eliminate reaching an "unbearable limit" in your classroom.

9) Learn to reward your students in more motivating ways. Learn why traditional reward systems actually set "traps" for future misbehavior. Learn strategies to detect and correct these problems by keeping your students intrinsically motivated.

10) "Hook" students with a wide array of prompting procedures. Master four basic prompting procedures that will put you at center stage when you need it. Engage the "easy to teach" as well as the "reluctant learner" with these simple yet powerful techniques.

District Trainings

• Four-Day "Train-The-Trainer" Series

For more than one decade, we have been presenting highly acclaimed and useful one- and two-day trainings and seminars to schools and districts.

Teachers are successfully using our strategies in tens of thousands of classrooms across America. We have also been training school staff to become expert Time To Teach trainers and facilitators within their very own schools and districts. We also offer a highly regarded, comprehensive, "train-the-trainer" four-day seminar.

Following this comprehensive four-day "train-the-trainer" seminar, we leave behind a group of expert Time To Teach resident teacher practitioners who are fully accredited to train our program in their respective districts – indefinitely. These accredited trainers are also granted adjunct faculty status and can provide training for college credit within their school district.

www.timetoteach.com & *www.goteachergo.com*

Federal and state mandates are strongly encouraging that schools participate in programs and trainings that are both effective and enduring. The effectiveness of our program speaks for itself, and as to the enduring component, our "train-the-trainer" course will ensure that the school and district will have highly capable trainers on staff and ready to train cutting-edge classroom- and school-wide management strategies for years and years to come.

Invitational Seminars

Offered yearly to teachers throughout the United States for college credit, and for state professional hours. Look for a seminar in your state at www.timetoteach.com.

Keynotes

Our presenters are also master teachers themselves. These elite, "active duty," K-12 teacher trainers are often asked to present our exciting concepts for conference, school, and district openings.

You will find this keynote both highly useful, and also very entertaining. Our innovative ideas are helping schools everywhere. Teachers begin the session with courteous giggles, move through open chuckles and into side-splitting belly laughs as our sought-after trainers share anecdotes, ideas, and most important, **solutions** to classroom effectiveness.

Training With Live Music?

We pay attention to the research! And we have plenty of it indicating that learning outcomes are significantly increased with the use of music.

We **optionally** offer some of our trainings with live music and meaningful lyrics that correspond to Time To Teach strategies! Your trainer, who is a master K-12 teacher with national recognition, presents Time To Teach strategies and ideas throughout the day. Music and lyrics specifically designed for the occasion and topic are intermittently performed throughout the day. You will laugh, cry, and be moved to learn like never before!

www.timetoteach.com & www.goteachergo.com

What you don't know yet, is that the music is performed by John Carswell, an internationally renowned musician who has performed with Ray Charles, BB King, and many other legends.

Simply put, there is nothing available like this...anywhere in education...period! It is amazingly informative and immensely entertaining, and unquestionably unique. Therefore, you will never forget it.

Realize, the training content does not change with the addition of music. The music accentuates the speakers topic, and believe us when we say that your teachers will report that this was the most useful **and** fun seminar they have ever attended.

In-Depth Materials Information

BOOKS

High Expectations and Winning Classroom Behavior
150 Essential Lesson Plans For Classroom Success!
by Rick Dahlgren

Availability: Available for immediate shipment

Complementary Materials
    ✓ *highly recommended for use with this book:*

Books
- Bell Work
- Moving From Ordinary to Extraordinary Relationships With Your Students: Creating A Classroom That All Love To Enter

DVD'S
- Time To Teach: Tools For Tomorrow *not just* Theory For Thought
- Self-Control: Remaining Cool and Responding Right!

www.timetoteach.com & www.goteachergo.com

- ◆ High Expectations and Winning Classroom Behavior: 150 Essential Lesson Plans For Classroom Success!
- ◆ Emergency Intervention!
- ◆ Moving From Ordinary to Extraordinary Relationships With Your Students: Creating A Classroom That All Love To Enter

Description

After nearly five years of collaborative research with teachers from around America, Rick Dahlgren has compiled over 150 classroom- and school-wide teach-to's that successful "active duty" teachers are using in diverse classrooms across America, Canada, and abroad! Whether you purchase this book in September – or May – you will be only days away from calming your classroom and improving the feeling tone so that both you and your students can function at peak performance. Elementary and secondary teach-to's are included for both in-class as well as "common areas" (out-of-class areas).

We strongly suggest that you consider the 150 Essential Lesson Plans For Classroom Success! DVD so that you may read and next watch this powerful process in action.

Bell Work
by Rick Dahlgren and Mary Kotnour

Availability: *Available for shipment on April 1, 2005.*

Complementary Materials – none recommended

Description

Do any of your students experience trouble transitioning from one activity to another? Do you ever have guests, parents, helpers, or others show up to your classroom unannounced? Do administrators, counselors, specialists, or other important school personnel ever need a moment of your time during class to discuss important matters? Do your activities or lessons ever end a bit sooner than you had planned?   The answer is, of course, yes to all of these questions, and the solution is here. **Bell Work!**

This great book includes hundreds of "sponge activities," and bell work activities that will keep primary through secondary students active, busy, happy, and learning during entry, transitions, interruptions, timing snafu's, and so many other occasions that can interrupt our teaching day.

Very nice to have on hand for substitutes, and also to have ready to go when you are being observed. These sponge activities ensure that active participation and learning continue no matter what the condition, and administrators are always pleased and impressed that you have such contingencies in place!

Moving From Ordinary to Extraordinary Relationships With Your Students
Creating A Classroom That All Love To Enter
by Rick Dahlgren

Availability: *Available for shipment on September 1, 2005*

Complementary Materials
✓ *highly recommended for use with this book:*

Books
◆ High Expectations and Winning Classroom Behavior: 150 Essential Lesson Plans For Classroom Success!
◆ Bell Work

DVD's
◆ Time To Teach: Tools for Tomorrow *not just* Theory For Thought
◆ Self-Control: Remaining Cool and Responding Right!
◆ High Expectations and Winning Classroom Behavior: 150 Essential Lesson Plans For Classroom Success!
◆ Emergency Intervention!
◆ Moving From Ordinary to Extraordinary Relationships With Your Students: Creating A Classroom That All Love To Enter

www.timetoteach.com & *www.goteachergo.com*

Description

Madeline Hunter told us that "Kids don't care how much you know until they know how much you care." She was right. If you doubt it, recall yourself as both a child, and a student. What would your life have been like without love and acceptance from your parents? How would you have done in school if your teachers had never interacted with you as a person? A basic human need is to be cared for and respected for who we are, regardless of our abilities or accomplishments.

The book objective is to teach you how to treat kids with dignity and kindness **and** how that will pay **big** dividends, to you the teacher!

We believe that the proper way for teachers to show children how much we care is to simultaneously show them unconditional positive regard and hold them accountable for learning appropriate behavior. This book is about showing positive regard. Don't skip it – in your reading or in your teaching!

Play Cool At School
by Mary Kotnour and Rick Dahlgren

Availability: Available for immediate shipment

Complementary Materials – none recommended

Description

Do you take your kids to recess? Do you ever have "duty?" Do your children ever come back to class frustrated, unhappy, or in trouble? Perhaps there wasn't anything fun to do or they were bored or…?

You've heard the saying "dead time is bad time." Within this book are hundreds of physical activities that you can organize at recess, during P.E., before or after school, on field trips, or on field day. The physical activities are all easy to administer, fun to play and many have a learning theme embedded in the activity.

Schools that use this resource report far fewer "incidents" on the playground and children love the activities. Teachers too, because the kids come back to class happy and ready to learn!

Time To Teach – Training Manual
"Tools for Tomorrow *not just* Theory For Thought"
by Rick Dahlgren

Availability: *Available for immediate shipment*

Complementary Materials
✓ *highly recommended for use with this book:*

Books
- High Expectations and Winning Classroom Behavior: 150 Essential Lesson Plans For Classroom Success
- Bell Work
- Moving From Ordinary to Extraordinary Relationships With Your Students: Creating A Classroom That All Love To Enter

DVD'S
- Time To Teach: Tools for Tomorrow *not just* Theory For Thought
- Self-Control: Remaining Cool and Responding Right!
- High Expectations and Winning Classroom Behavior: 150 Essential Lesson Plans For Classroom Success
- Emergency Intervention!
- Moving From Ordinary to Extraordinary Relationships With Your Students: Creating A Classroom That All Love To Enter

Description
*NOTE – This training manual is distributed only to teachers and schools that participate in our trainings. It is not a "stand alone" book, and therefore requires work by the participant to "complete" it during our full-day trainings.

www.timetoteach.com & www.goteachergo.com

DVD'S

Time To Teach
"Tools for Tomorrow *not just* Theory For Thought"
with Rick Dahlgren and other master teachers

Availability: *Available for immediate shipment*

Complementary Materials
   ✓ *highly recommended for use with this DVD:*

Books
- High Expectations and Winning Classroom Behavior: 150 Essential Lesson Plans For Classroom Success
- Bell Work
- Moving From Ordinary to Extraordinary Relationships With Your Students: Creating A Classroom That All Love To Enter

DVD'S
- Self-Control: Remaining Cool and Responding Right!
- High Expectations and Winning Classroom Behavior: 150 Essential Lesson Plans For Classroom Success
- Emergency Intervention!
- Moving From Ordinary to Extraordinary Relationships With Your Students: Creating A Classroom That All Love To Enter

Description
Every strategy, idea, and detail in this book come to life in the Time To Teach DVD. Use another modality, now, to enhance your understanding of the powerful program strategies, and details. Watch and listen to leading teachers teach the strategies and ideas you learned in this book, and listen to real life classroom stories that help cement your understanding of the techniques you have learned.

Listen to questions from teachers from around America, and even better…listen to the answers from leading teachers who have been using this program for decades!

www.timetoteach.com & *www.goteachergo.com*

Self-Control: Remaining Cool and Responding Right!
"How to take the right course of action when being challenged"
with Rick Dahlgren

Availability: *Available for shipment on April 1, 2005*

Complementary Materials
✓ highly recommended for use with this DVD:

Books
♦ High Expectations and Winning Classroom Behavior: 150
   Essential Lesson Plans For Classroom Success
♦ Bell Work
♦ Moving From Ordinary to Extraordinary Relationships With Your
   Students: Creating A Classroom That All Love To Enter

DVD'S
♦ Time To Teach: Tools for Tomorrow *not just* Theory For Thought
♦ High Expectations and Winning Classroom Behavior: 150
   Essential Lesson Plans For Classroom Success
♦ Emergency Intervention!
♦ Moving From Ordinary to Extraordinary Relationships With Your
   Students: Creating A Classroom That All Love To Enter

Description
Do you know a teacher that never gets frustrated? He or she always remains in control of his or her emotions and faculties. Have you noticed how his or her classroom – the ethos – is also calm and respectful, and the children also seem unusually serene?

Great news for you! The strategies that this "with it" teacher uses are all learned behaviors and you are only minutes away from being the most composed and professional teacher in your building. Learn:
1) Why silence is powerful and calm is contagious
2) How to set limits (the three key elements)
3) About personal space and how not to "violate and agitate"

4) To use the "four phrases" that immediately take you away from confrontation...**every single time!**
5) How to detect and avoid threats, ultimatums, button pushing, past history comments, and more.

High Expectations and Winning Classroom Behavior
150 Essential Lesson Plans For Classroom Success
by Rick Dahlgren

Availability: Available for shipment on April 1, 2005

Complementary Materials
✓ *highly recommended for use with this DVD:*

Books
◆ High Expectations and Winning Classroom Behavior: 150 Essential Lesson Plans For Classroom Success
◆ Bell Work
◆ Moving From Ordinary to Extraordinary Relationships With Your Students: Creating A Classroom That All Love To Enter

DVD'S
◆ Time To Teach: Tools for Tomorrow *not just* Theory For Thought
◆ Self-Control: Remaining Cool and Responding Right!
◆ Emergency Intervention!
◆ Moving From Ordinary to Extraordinary Relationships With Your Students: Creating A Classroom That All Love To Enter

Description
After nearly five years of collaborative research with teachers from around America, Rick Dahlgren has compiled over 150 classroom- and school-wide teach-to's that successful "active duty" teachers are using in diverse classrooms across America, Canada, and abroad! We suggest you buy and read the book: High Expectations and Winning Classroom Behavior, first, and then watch this DVD.

www.timetoteach.com & www.goteachergo.com

Whether you purchase this DVD in September – or May – you will be only days away from calming your classroom and improving the feeling tone so that both you and your students will function at peak performance.

Specific details for teaching-to expectations and routines for elementary and secondary students are included. Also included are instructions on how to give children a "voice" in the development of your rules. Research tells us that if children have a "voice" in the development of classroom rules, two things happen:
1) They are more likely to follow the rules
2) They are more likely to take the "consequence" if they break the rules (because they helped make them!)

Emergency Intervention!
"Five Immediate Action Steps To Take When Confronted By The Verbally or Physically Aggressive Student!"
with Rick Dahlgren

Availability: Available for shipment on April 1, 2005

Complementary Materials

✓ *highly recommended for use with this DVD:*

Books
♦ High Expectations and Winning Classroom Behavior: 150 Essential Lesson Plans For Classroom Success
♦ Bell Work
♦ Moving From Ordinary to Extraordinary Relationships With Your Students: Creating A Classroom That All Love To Enter

DVD'S
♦ Time To Teach: Tools for Tomorrow *not just* Theory For Thought
♦ Self-Control: Remaining Cool and Responding Right!
♦ High Expectations and Winning Classroom Behavior: 150 Essential Lesson Plans For Classroom Success
♦ Moving From Ordinary to Extraordinary Relationships With Your Students: Creating A Classroom That All Love To Enter

www.timetoteach.com & www.goteachergo.com

Page 146

Description

Have you, or a teaching colleague, ever had a child removed from a classroom? Did it look good?

Often, the principal is the person we ask for help. And the minute you do that you have just reinforced the old "wait until dad gets home" scenario, and the student witnesses you giving your credibility away to the principal to "take care of matters."

Let us teach you the "Five Immediate Action Steps To Take When Confronted By The Verbally or Physically Aggressive Student." Let us also teach you how to organize a "crack team" of "happy, smiling, teaching professionals" to positively respond to any event, at any time, in any building. Let us teach you how to do this in a nonconfrontational manner, and how to be successful every single time!

This process has been field tested in the "toughest" schools and it almost always works!

Time To Teach – School-Wide DVD
Tools for Tomorrow *not just* Theory For Thought
with Rick Dahlgren and other master teachers

Availability: *Available for immediate shipment*

Complementary Materials
✓ *highly recommended for use with this DVD:*

Books
♦ Time To Teach – Training Manual "Tools for Tomorrow *not just* Theory For Thought"
♦ High Expectations and Winning Classroom Behavior: 150 Essential Lesson Plans For Classroom Success
♦ Bell Work
♦ Moving From Ordinary to Extraordinary Relationships With Your Students: Creating A Classroom That All Love To Enter
♦ Play Cool At School

www.timetoteach.com & *www.goteachergo.com*

DVD'S
- Self-Control: Remaining Cool and Responding Right!
- High Expectations and Winning Classroom Behavior: 150 Essential Lesson Plans For Classroom Success
- Emergency Intervention!
- Moving From Ordinary to Extraordinary Relationships With Your Students: Creating A Classroom That All Love To Enter

CD
- Teachin' The Blues Away

Description
*NOTE – This DVD is only distributed to schools who have been trained by the Center For Teacher Effectiveness, or one of its trainers. Sorry, no exceptions.

This package is loaded with practical ideas and powerful ideas that you learned during your staff development. It is designed to help you and your staff remember and revisit Time To Teach strategies for years to come. **The set is consists of over 25 discs.** It includes:

- All of the Self-Control strategies you have learned, which will help you "Remain Calm and Respond Right" every time.

- All of the Teach-To philosophy and strategies, which will help set you and your children up for peak performance.

- All of the Unconditional Positive Regard philosophy and strategies which will help you establish connections with all children, even children who challenge, and which always pay big dividends to the classroom teacher.

- All of the REFOCUS philosophy and strategies which will guarantee that you "stay out of the tornado" and never again find yourself giving multiple warnings and repeated requests.

- All of the critically important "what if's" asked by teachers from around America, and answered by a master educator.

www.timetoteach.com & www.goteachergo.com

- Actual footage of REFOCUSING students (real events) with narration.

- The "Emergency Intervention" series is included, which will help you and your staff respond calmly, powerfully, and responsibly to any tense situation that arises in your classroom or school. Learn the "Five Immediate Action Steps To Take When Confronted By The Verbally or Physically Aggressive Student."

- A parent DVD "Time To Teach – Time To Parent." This DVD describes the Time To Teach program in easy to understand terms for the parent, introduces the notion of Teach-To's, Unconditional Positive Regard, and the REFOCUS process. This is truly a public relations bonanza for your school. After reviewing the DVD, it is apparent that your staff has embarked on a positive program with only one intent – which is to provide and promote a positive, safe, high performing learning atmosphere.

- Twenty (20) "crash course" substitute CD's (or comparable discs) to leave in every classroom. Never again leave the substitute out of the "discipline loop."

CD

Just for fun! Produced and written by Rick Dahlgren. Music by internationally renowned blues artist John Carswell. John has performed with Ray Charles, Ike and Tina Turner, BB King & many other legends! This musical CD was designed to help Time To Teach participants remember what they learned during our training. The music is fun, and the lyrics are written just for teachers. It is a one of a kind item!

Order Form On Next Page!

Order Form

1) Specify <u>Quantity</u> and 2) compute <u>Total</u> for each line item.

Qty	Book Title	Price	Total
	High Expectations and Winning Classroom Behavior	$39.00	$
	Play Cool At School	$49.00	$
	Bell Work	$25.00	$
	"…From Ordinary To Extraordinary Relationships…"	$25.00	$
	Time To Teach – Training Manual	$25.00	$

Qty	DVD Title	Price	Total
	Time To Teach – The Program on DVD (5+ hours)	$149.00	$
	Self-Control – Remaining Cool and Responding Right	$45.00	$
	High Expectations and Winning Classroom Behavior	$45.00	$
	Emergency Intervention!	$45.00	$
	"…From Ordinary To Extraordinary Relationships…"	$35.00	$
	Time To Teach – School-Wide DVD (8+ hours)	$900.00	$

Qty	CD		
	Teachin' The Blues Away	$12.00	$

Grand Total (add all item totals) → $

2) Complete this "ship to" section: Send payment to:

Where should we ship your materials?	Mail or Fax Order Form To:
My Name	
Address	*Center For Teacher Effectiveness*
City	*4381 English Point Road*
State	*Hayden Lake, ID 83835*
Zip	*(fax) 208-762-7026*
Tel: ( )	*(tel) 208-772-0273*
Email	

3) Method of Payment (check one below)

☐ Am.Ex. ☐ Discover ☐ VISA ☐ MC ☐ PO ☐ Check ☐ Bill Me (see below)

CC # _____ expiration date _____

Your Signature_____

NOTE* If choosing the "bill me" option you must furnish your drivers license number and fax or mail a copy of the front of your license along with this order form.
Drivers license # _____

www.timetoteach.com & *www.goteachergo.com*